Fabergé

# FABERGÉ

## Virginia Museum of Fine Arts

by David Park Curry
Curator of American Arts

with the assistance of
Caroline Doswell Smith
and Mark Sprinkle

Library of Congress Cataloging-in-Publication Data
Virginia Museum of Fine Arts.
     Fabergé : Virginia Museum of Fine Arts / David Park Curry,
  with the assistance of Caroline Doswell Smith and Mark Sprinkle.
     p.    cm.
     Includes bibliographical references and index.
     ISBN 0-917046-40-4
     1. Fabergé, Peter Carl, 1846–1920—Catalogs.  2. Faberzhe
(Firm)—Catalogs.  3. Jewelry—Russia—Catalogs.  4. Art objects,
Russian—Catalogs.  5. Pratt, Lillian Thomas, B. 1876?—Art col-
lections—Catalogs.  6. Jewelry—Virginia—Richmond—Catalogs.
7. Art objects—Virginia—Richmond—Catalogs.  8. Virginia
Museum of Fine Arts—Catalogs.  I. Curry, David Park.  II. Smith,
Caroline Doswell.  III. Sprinkle, Mark.  IV. Title.
NK7398.F32A4  1995
739.2'092—dc20                          95-20926
                                              CIP

ISBN 0-917046-40-4
Printed in the United States of America

Produced by the Office of Publications, Virginia Museum of Fine Arts,
   2800 Grove Avenue, Richmond, Virginia 23221-2466 USA
Photographs of Virginia Museum of Fine Arts Collections
   by Katherine Wetzel, Richmond
Edited by Anne B. Barriault
Book Design by Sarah Lavicka
Composed by the designer in QuarkXpress. Type set in Centaur
   with italics in Sabon.
Printed on acid-free 80 lb. Warren Lustro Enamel Dull text by
   Carter Printing, Richmond. Binding by Advantage Book Binding,
   Inc., Glen Burnie, Maryland.

FRONT AND BACK COVERS: *Peter Carl Fabergé's* **Imperial Czarevich Easter Egg,** *1912, and* **Miniature Easter Eggs** *from the Fabergé Workshops, Virginia Museum of Fine Arts, Bequest from the Estate of Lillian Thomas Pratt (Checklist Numbers 4 and 42a–42s).*

FRONTISPIECE: **Five Fabulous Fabergé Eggs,** *pictured here in relative sizes, crown the Lillian Thomas Pratt Collection at the Virginia Museum of Fine Arts (Checklist Numbers 1 to 5).*

TABLE OF CONTENTS: *Fabergé's* **Scarab Brooch** *from the Pratt Collection, Virginia Museum of Fine Arts (Checklist Number 6).*

FACING p. vii, FOREWORD: *Literally fit for a queen: Fabergé's* **Champagne Flute.** *Virginia Museum of Fine Arts, Bequest of Lelia Blair Northrop (Checklist Number 7).*

# CONTENTS

A Toast to Mrs. Pratt

# FOREWORD

Imagination and delight are vital ingredients in life, in creative expression, *and* in art museums! The wit and elegance lavished on the Fabergé jewels within these pages are hallmarks of the permanent collections of the Virginia Museum of Fine Arts. Our jewels can be found beyond these tangible treasures, however; and so this book is dedicated with heartfelt thanks for gems of inspiration and funding to

## The Council of the Virginia Museum of Fine Arts.

We are especially grateful to Virginia Museum of Fine Arts contributors who have provided additional funding for this publication:

## The Julia Louise Reynolds Fund for American Decorative Arts

## The June Mohr Memorial Fund

## The Leslie Cheek, Jr., Publications Endowment.

Each has helped to ensure the Museum's commitment to excellence in the fine arts. Special recognition is also due our curator of American art, David Park Curry, for this presentation of the Museum's collection of beloved jewels—the Fabergé objects—and their donor, Mrs. Pratt.

KATHARINE C. LEE
Director
Virginia Museum of Fine Arts

vii

# PREFACE

When you touch or hold a Fabergé object, you are in contact with something, coming down to you, not only from the era of the Czars, but of an ancestry far more ancient; for it is typical of all the imperial courts there have ever been.

Sacheverell Sitwell, 1949

Few of us have the opportunity to hold one of Peter Carl Fabergé's imperial Easter gifts, to feel the cool, self-assured enamel surface, to scrutinize the intricacies of the delicate metalwork, to count the rose-cut diamonds or cabochon rubies or seed pearls scattered like grace notes across the rounded, substantial form, and finally, to pop open the shell and carefully extract the glittering prize. Yet, since Lillian Thomas Pratt left the Virginia Museum of Fine Arts her collection of Fabergé, crowned by five imperial Easter eggs, thousands of Museumgoers have touched these exquisite pieces with their eyes, owned them in their imaginations.

Mrs. Pratt's extensive bequest of jeweled and enameled treasures from the Fabergé Workshops entered the Museum in 1947 amid a flurry of national publicity. Her gift remains the most readily recognized of the many types of collections now under the Museum's care. Celebrated as a "Royal Haul" by *Time* magazine, Mrs. Pratt's Fabergé pieces were augmented by her donation of related Russian decorative arts, including icons and textiles, and later by the fiscal support of her widowed husband, John Lee Pratt. The couple's generosity quickly established the Virginia Museum of Fine Arts as one of the largest and best-known repositories for such material outside Russia.

Half a century later, the collection still maintains a high profile. Each year gallery visitors, young and old alike, steadily stream past the Fabergé cases, savoring the charm of these exquisitely wrought imperial treasures. Shortly after the Pratt collection was given to the Commonwealth, Sacheverell Sitwell introduced the first thorough biography of Peter Carl Fabergé (Bainbridge 1949). His evocative commentary captures in print something of the magic that invests these eggs, boxes, picture frames, cups, handles, seals, and hardstone figures with lasting appeal—they let us reach into a past that shines all the more resplendent for its very remoteness from everyday experience.

A flood of books, exhibition catalogues, and articles on the Fabergé Workshops is now available. Writers on the topic tend to include many lists: imperial Easter eggs and their dates; groups of similar objects such as umbrella handles or hardstone animals; names and marks of Fabergé workmasters; names of previous owners; significant historical events in Fabergé's firm; public collections where Fabergé pieces can be seen. All these lists name bits of Fabergé's legacy, helping us to gain a hold on his treasures, to sift with the mind what cannot be touched with the fingers. As English novelist Nancy Mitford once wrote, "the pill of historical research is gilded with the primitive and universal excitement of a treasure hunt."

The purpose of this little book is to take readers on a visual treasure hunt, letting them explore parts of the Lillian Thomas Pratt collection afresh, concentrating on some of the less familiar fragments of her story, giving a wider context to the anomaly of a Russian royal collection in an American public museum. The historical pill is gilded with exciting new photography that brings to life some of the easily missed design details orchestrated by Fabergé and his workers into such memorable objects of desire.

DAVID PARK CURRY
Curator of American Arts
Virginia Museum of Fine Arts

# ACKNOWLEDGMENTS

Whenever my grandmother did something especially nice for me she would say, "I wish it were emeralds." My thanks always seemed inadequate. So do they now, as I try to acknowledge the multitude of friends and colleagues who have contributed to this complex yet most enjoyable project. Some eighteen months ago, when I first opened up the Fabergé file cabinet at the Virginia Museum of Fine Arts, it seemed like a Pandora's box. Now the relevant object files are organized, our Fabergé pieces beautifully conserved and photographed, our archival material pulled together, and our understanding of Lillian Thomas Pratt, an unusual and generous collector, rests on fact rather than anecdote.

Many people have had a hand in the project. If each one who contributed to the creation of this little book were a precious stone, the gems would make a necklace to rival the "King's Ransom" celebrated by Armand Hammer in his *Quest of the Romanoff Treasure*. The sparkling trove includes:

RUBIES FOR RESEARCH: Virginia Museum of Fine Arts curatorial assistant Caroline Doswell Smith; research assistant Mark Sprinkle; summer interns Allison McClintic and Catherine Farish; archivist Jennie Runnels and library assistant Elizabeth Yevich; registration information analyst Mary Sullivan; photographic resources manager Howell Perkins; and docent M. T. Grund. Fabergé scholars Géza von Habsburg, New York; Anne Odom, Hillwood; Marilyn Swezey, Washington, D.C.; Russian specialists Elena Balashova, Berkeley; David Griffiths, University of North Carolina, Chapel Hill; George Munro, and Natasha Chernyak, Virginia Commonwealth University; Elena Varshavskaya, St. Petersburg; and musician Mary Boodell, Richmond.

PEARLS FOR PRESERVATION: Conservator Carol Aiken, Baltimore. Virginia Museum of Fine Arts objects conservator Larry Becker; objects conservation fellow Ellen Salzman; objects conservation technician Amy Fernandez.

EMERALDS FOR EDITING: Virginia Museum of Fine Arts senior editor Anne B. Barriault; series editor and publications manager Monica S. Rumsey; publications production coordinator Amy Van Buren.

DIAMONDS FOR DESIGN: Virginia Museum of Fine Arts chief graphic designer Sarah Lavicka. Photographer Katherine Wetzel, Richmond.

SAPPHIRES FOR SUPPORT: Virginia Museum of Fine Arts Director Katharine C. Lee; deputy director, Carol Amato; associate director, communications and marketing, Michael Smith; associate registrar Maureen Morrisette, and head registrar Lisa Hancock; art handler Roy Thompson; photographer Denise Lewis; associate director, exhibitions and planning, Richard B. Woodward;

collections office manager Mitzie Booth; executive secretaries Caryl Burtner, Diana Dougherty, and Michelle Wilson; and systems administrator, Robert Enroughty.

AQUAMARINES FOR ADVICE: John Curtis, Williamsburg; Lee Hunt Miller, Ann Karlstrom, and Karen Kevorkian, The Fine Arts Museums of San Francisco; Ira Spanierman, New York; Diana Edwards, Baltimore; Mrs. Bowlman T. Bowles, Jr., Dr. Herbert A. Claiborne, Jr., Mrs. Alan S. Donnahoe, Mrs. David C. Durrill, Joseph T. Knox, Anna Noyes, Mrs. Richard S. Reynolds III, Marianne Svoboda, and Sally Todd, Richmond; and Patricia Draher and Suzanne Kotz, Seattle.

Of course, no necklace is complete without a dependable clasp. G. Rebecca is mine, so the Orlov diamond (194 1/2 carats) would be redundant.

— D.P.C.

*A King's Ransom on a Single Table: salvaged Romanov treasures illustrated by entrepreneur Armand Hammer in the 1930s.*

**Note to the Reader:**

Familiar Russian words (*czar*) and names (for example, Nicholas and Alexis) are anglicized. Others generally follow a modified Library of Congress transliteration system (for example, Nikolaevich and Aleksandrovna).

Illustrations are designated as follows: (NO. 1) through (NO. 42) refer to the Fabergé, European, and Russian Decorative Arts Collections in the Virginia Museum of Fine Arts; the reader will find more information about these objects, listed by number, in the *Checklist*, pp. 107–13. All other illustrations are numbered (FIG. 1) through (FIG. 27); photography credits may be found on p. 118.

Authors and dates of publications cited in the following chapters are enclosed in parentheses—for example (Lesley 1976)—and are keyed to references in *A Fabergé Bookshelf*, p. 115.

# CHAPTER I

# IN A MIRRORED CABINET:

## History of a Collection

In a gently wistful memorial portrait commissioned by her husband almost a quarter
of a century after her death, Lillian Thomas
Pratt hovers on the bank of the Rappahannock, across the river from Fredericksburg,
Virginia (FIG. I). Her cut-stone bench is
the most substantial object in an otherwise
gauzy composition. One might not guess
from this ethereal image, based on a turn-
of-the-century family photograph, that Mrs.
Pratt's determined pursuit of Russian decorative arts established her among the leading
American collectors of Fabergé.

I

FIG. I. *Julien Binford's posthumous*
***Portrait of Lillian Thomas Pratt****,*
*Virginia Museum of Fine Arts.*

Almost ghostly in her filmy white dress, she is surrounded by a haze of mauve, pink, and blue that recalls shimmering enamels on some of the Fabergé pieces she collected from 1933 until 1945. As our research began, Mrs. Pratt's story was similarly obscured in a haze of legends. She was little more than a ghost, really—someone thought to have gathered fabulous hoards of Russian treasures almost unnoticed, hiding them away in hatboxes and shoe boxes until they were suddenly visited upon the Virginia Museum of Fine Arts as an unexpected bequest in 1947.

Almost fifty years later, archival evidence of a large mirrored cabinet came to light. The four-by-six-foot cabinet was one of several pieces of furniture expressly designed for Chatham Manor, the Pratt's house on the Rappahannock, to display the family's Fabergé treasures in all their sparkling glory. Available evidence reflects a Mrs. Pratt quite different from the one hovering in the posthumous portrait. Mrs. Pratt was a woman of substance and purpose—the history of her collection offers a tale as compelling as any legend.

## PETRO PRIMO, CATHARINA SECUNDA FABERGÉ TERTIO

By the time the young Peter Carl Fabergé completed his studies in Dresden and Frankfurt, returning to St. Petersburg between 1864 and 1866 to enter his father's jewelry firm, a tradition of eclectic splendor was already well established in the Russia of the Romanovs. Soon after Peter the Great gained a seaport by founding a new capital on the marshy banks of the Neva River in 1703, the imperial court at St. Petersburg began its steady patronage of architects, artists, and artisans who drew their inspiration from seemingly disparate cultures, looking simultaneously eastward to the riches of Asia and westward to the high points of Renaissance, Baroque, and Rococo art and architecture.

FIG. 2. *Peter the Great*: *a famous landmark in St. Petersburg since 1782.*

3

As a cultural and a political leader, Catherine the Great followed in Peter's footsteps. The memorial statue she commissioned to honor her illustrious predecessor is inscribed, "Petro Primo/ Catharina Secunda" (FIG. 2). While Peter had instituted Russia's first public museum, the Museum of Natural History, Catherine went further, amassing vast numbers of Old Master paintings and sculpture, to place the collections of the Russian court on a par with German, French, and English counterparts. In the course of Catherine's reign, the buildings now collectively known as the State Hermitage began to appear along the banks of the Neva River.

Many of the works of art Catherine acquired became more accessible during Fabergé's lifetime when, under Nicholas I, the New Hermitage opened its doors to the public in 1852. Public museums were soon to become important design repositories for the arts of preceding eras. During the second half of the nineteenth century, objects in museums served to inspire architects, painters, and designers as a series of stylistic revivals swept through international art circles. Fabergé is known to have based some of his work upon earlier objects, after studying treasures in various museums, including the famed Grünes Gewölbe (Green Vaults) of Dresden, and his employees at the Fabergé Workshops were particularly skilled at creative historicism. Historicizing designs initially brought the firm to wider public attention with exhibits like the prize-winning gold replica of the Scythian Treasure, made by workmaster Erik Kollin for the Nuremberg Fine Art Exhibition in 1885.

At about this time, the firm began making *objets de fantaisie*—little luxuries that were both useful and beautiful—and that would eventually make Fabergé a household name. Whether elegantly restrained or of barbarian richness, Fabergé's objects display a sophisticated interweaving of design elements distilled from several centuries of goldmasters' and jewelers' arts. A tiny gold *Egg Nécessaire* now in the Pratt collection recalls the once-indispensible needle-

N O . 8 . *Fabergé's **Egg Nécessaire**, inspired by earlier needle-and-scissor cases.*

and-scissor cases of eighteenth-century France (NO. 8). A minuscule gilt silver *Bonbonnière*, whose delicious canary-yellow enamel is sparked with diamonds, rubies, and pearls, imitates a Louis XVI sweetbox (NO. 9). François Petrovich Birbaum, one of Fabergé's head workmasters, recalled in his memoirs that "the eighteenth-century works of art in

NO. 9. *Fabergé's **Bonbonnière** recalls candy boxes of the 1700s.*

the Hermitage inspired the use of transparent enamel on engraved and guilloched gold and silver" (Birbaum 1919).

The House of Fabergé served the last three Russian imperial courts, ruled by Czars Alexander II (reigned: 1855–1881), Alexander III (reigned: 1881–1894), and Nicholas II (reigned: 1896–1917). Their extravagant regimes ensured a continuing demand for luxurious *objets de vertu*, such as umbrella handles and picture frames. The St. Petersburg shop was always crowded, Birbaum recalled:

> The Grand Dukes and Duchesses . . . spent a long time choosing their purchases. Every day from four to five all the Petersburg aristocracy could be seen there: the titled, the civil service, and the commercial. In Holy Week these rendezvous were particularly crowded as everyone hurried to buy the traditional Easter eggs and . . . to glance at the egg made for the Emperor.

Fabergé's roster of clients went far beyond the crowned heads of Europe to include well-heeled commoners worldwide. He could never have satisfied their demands all alone. Just as Peter the Great set out a general plan for the architectural ensembles of St. Petersburg, so Peter Carl Fabergé, taking over the family firm in 1872, oversaw, but did not actually make, most of the objects sold through his shops in St. Petersburg, Moscow, Odessa, Kiev, and London. Nor did he invent decorative eggs as Easter gifts; their presentation was already a long-established tradition in Europe. Instead, alive to what was all around him, Fabergé reworked the multifaceted heritage of the Russian past.

NO. 3. *A Rococo cartouche on Fabergé's* **Peter the Great Egg.**

FIG. 4. *Rococo wall-moldings in a St. Petersburg palace.*

7

The self-involved voluptuousness of Fabergé Workshop productions settles into perspective when we consider how their obsessive components miniaturize the fantastical colors, textures, and forms of traditional Russian architecture (FIG. 3). A tiny portrait affixed to the shell of an imperial Easter egg is surrounded by a golden cartouche, echoing the gilded Rococo moldings that encrust the walls of the Catherine Palace at Tsarskoe Selo, the imperial summer residence, and other palaces in and around St. Petersburg (NO. 3, FIG. 4).

FIG. 3. *Decorative domes, like extravagant eggs, capture the spirit of traditional Russian architecture during Fabergé's heyday.*

In general, when the Fabergé Workshops produced images of Nicholas and his family to decorate or fill some of the eggs commissioned by the Czar, they miniaturized long-established patterns of European royal portraiture (FIG. 7). Interspersed with portraits of the Czar, Czarina, their four daughters, and their only son are tiny history paintings that capture such events as a procession to Uspensky Cathedral, or the unveilings of a monument commemorating the Battle of Poltava or a statue of Peter the Great at Riga. Such a cycle has its historical counterpart in enormous royal paintings such as Jacques-Louis David's uncompleted series for the Luxembourg Palace to commemorate the reign of Napoleon Bonaparte (FIGS. 5, 6).

8

FIG. 5. *Vasily Zuiev's coronation of Czar Nicholas II occupies barely a square inch (detail).* **Fifteenth Anniversary Egg,** *1911. The* FORBES *Magazine Collection, New York.*

FIG. 6. *Jacques-Louis David's* **Coronation of Napoleon and Josephine** *measures 20 by 30 feet (detail), 1805–7. The Louvre Museum, Paris.*

FIG. 7. *Russian empress Catherine the Great strolls in the garden at Tsarskoe Selo, in Vladimir Borovikovsky's royal portrait. The State Russian Museum, St. Petersburg.*

FIG. 8. *The **First Imperial Egg,** made in traditional form but of precious materials for the Empress Maria, Czar Nicholas's mother, 1885. The FORBES Magazine Collection, New York.*

With its white enamel shell, golden yolk, and hidden hen—which opens to reveal a piece of jewelry—the first documented imperial egg (1885) closely followed European precedents for suitable Easter gifts (FIG. 8). But the imperial eggs soon took on topical significance, for variety in the face of such a well-established tradition was no easy task. Birbaum recalled:

> Novelty was achieved with great difficulty, and everyone had had more than enough of trying. When roused, old Mr. Fabergé [Peter Carl's father, Gustav] was not noticeably restrained. He innocently declared…that in two weeks' time he would be finishing work on square eggs. Some of the people standing around smiled, others were discomfited, but [one] lady did not grasp the point. As if that were not enough, she actually came to the shop in two weeks' time to buy these eggs. The old man explained to her quite seriously that he had hoped to produce them but had been unsuccessful.

Demands on the firm's ingenuity doubled after the coronation of Nicholas II in 1896, when imperial Easter gifts were commissioned for both his wife, Czarina Alexandra, and his mother, Dowager Empress Maria. Orders from wealthy commoners, such as Siberian tycoon Alexander Ferdinandovich Kelch, further taxed the designers' imaginations.

Gradually the everyday lives and accomplishments of the Romanovs began to furnish themes for individual Easter gifts. Many of the surviving imperial eggs, including Mrs. Pratt's *Czarevich Egg* (NO. 4) and *Red Cross Egg* (NO. 5), contain family portraits. Others focus on royal residences. A golden palace—the

FIG. 9. *Gatchina Palace Egg*, about 1902.
*The Walters Art Gallery, Baltimore.*

dowager empress's favorite—is all the more impressive for its diminutive scale. An inch high, it fills the *Gatchina Palace Egg*, given to her about 1902 (FIG. 9). Miniature paintings of various palaces, summer houses, and official buildings fill several more, including the *Rock Crystal Egg* (NO. 1) and the *Pelican Egg* (NO. 2), both in the Pratt collection. At times miniature paintings of buildings embellish a shell, as does the Winter Palace on Mrs. Pratt's *Peter the Great Egg* (NO. 3). Some gifts, like the *Trans-Siberian Railway Egg* (1901, Armory Museum, Moscow) celebrate technological achievements; others, such as the *Fifteenth Anniversary Egg* (1911, FIG. 5, detail), commemorate major events during Czar Nicholas II's reign, a familiar kind of royal commission.

The visual texture of St. Petersburg, the Babylon of the Snows, provided glittering grist for Fabergé's design mill. For example, a miniature of the Peter the Great statue rises like clockwork from the interior of a golden egg encrusted with rubies and diamonds, made in 1903 to celebrate St. Petersburg's bicentennial (NO. 3). The inscription from the monumental statue—"Petro Primo/Catharina Secunda"—is repeated in tiny letters cut into a block of sapphire that supports the tiny horseman. While "Nicholas Tertio" is implied by both the decorative program of this egg and the Czar who commissioned it, Nicholas II was an ill-fated ruler almost completely out of touch with his constituency (Radzinsky 1992). "Fabergé Tertio" might have been more appropriate. Hindsight lets us suggest that the Fabergé Workshops—more

NO. 3. *The surprise hidden inside the **Peter the Great Egg**: a tiny version of St. Petersburg's famous statue.*

13

than almost anything else—have kept the Romanovs, particularly Nicholas and Alexandra, household names. Their continuing currency in American popular culture rests, in part, upon collections like the one formed by Lillian Thomas Pratt.

# AN AESTHETIC ANTIQUARIAN

Mrs. Pratt bequeathed about five hundred items to the Virginia Museum of Fine Arts. Eighty percent of the collection is Russian decorative art, much of it by the Fabergé Workshops. Like two of the other most important American collectors of the 1930s and 1940s—Marjorie Merriweather Post and India Early Minshall—Mrs. Pratt's interests went beyond Fabergé jeweled enamels and hard-

FIG. 10. *Lillian Thomas Pratt with her husband in their Chatham Manor garden, about 1933.*

stones to include embroidered textiles as well as both antique and modern icons. American paintings and furniture, a few Chinese jades, even some Egyptian antiquities also figure in Mrs. Pratt's famous legacy.

Today, however, the donor is as enigmatic as her collection is well known. Both Mr. and Mrs. Pratt were extremely private indi-viduals—old friends recall them as publicity-shy. A rare snapshot records the couple in the garden of their historic Fredericksburg house (FIG. 10). The photograph captures the no-nonsense posture of the former farm lad later praised by a General Motors president as "the best businessman I have ever known," as well as the reassuring solidity of the private secretary who became his wife.

A self-made multimillionaire, Mr. Pratt retired in 1937 to devote himself to various philanthropic causes, assiduously avoiding the limelight. Access to reliable personal information about the couple is limited, and conflicting data has been published. We do know that Mrs. Pratt was probably born in 1876 in Philadelphia; that by 1893 she had moved with her mother to Tacoma, Washington; and that she worked as a stenographer at the Puget Sound Flouring Mill by 1900. By 1917, she had married her second husband, John Lee Pratt, who "came to Tacoma in 1907 as a $100-a-month engineer," according to a Seattle newspaper (FIG. 11).

Endearing anecdotes help to shed a bit of light on the

FIG. 11. *Mr. and Mrs. Pratt, about 1917, shortly after their marriage.*

FIG. 12. *Mr. and Mrs. Pratt in a mid-1930s publicity shot for
a subsidiary of General Motors.*

enigmatic couple. The Pratts were not without a humorous sense
of irony. A carefully posed photograph from the mid 1930s shows
Mrs. Pratt looking on as her husband prepares to fry an egg
(FIG. 12). Mrs. Pratt's household datebooks give the impression
that she was a sociable person, actively engaged in community
affairs; a familiar figure in the Rappahannock Valley Garden Club;
a woman fond of cards, cocktail parties, and going to the movies.

In a newspaper interview, Mr. Pratt's niece recalled that her uncle kept trim by taking lengthy walks around Fredericksburg and declined to accept rides, whatever the weather:

> One stormy evening Mrs. Pratt and her housekeeper were driving across the bridge in a cold rain when Mrs. Pratt saw a figure leaning into the wind. "Look at that poor old man!" she exclaimed. "Let's offer him a ride." "That poor old man is Mr. Pratt," said the housekeeper. "Drive on," said Mrs. Pratt.

However, Mrs. Pratt was not always conveyed in the chauffeured 1933 Cadillac V-8 limousine, with optional hard spare-wheel hood and stylish new "spinner" wheel-covers, visible in the garden snapshot (FIG. 10). Lillian Thomas Pratt was born in Philadelphia as the United States celebrated its centennial with an international exhibition there, marking the nation's coming of age as a great industrial world power. She was married the year that the extravagant Romanov dynasty fell. Like her husband, she embodies a central component of the American dream: hard work rewarded. Her collecting habits echo patterns of consumption established in America during the last quarter of the nineteenth century.

NO. 10. *Fabergé's rock crystal globe traveled half the world to become part of Mrs. Pratt's collection.*

Nonetheless, a general tendency to romanticize Fabergé still tinges stories of how Mrs. Pratt formed her collection. Over the years, like a game of "telephone," variations on the theme of an eccentric woman using "pin money" to squirrel away a hoard of sparkling Russian trinkets right under her husband's nose have been constructed from available tidbits and legitimized in print. One version suggested that Mrs. Pratt concealed her collection in her bedroom closet: "Upon Lillian Pratt's death, her husband, who had known little of the Fabergé collection, found it stuffed in hatboxes" (Rouse 1985). Other versions assume that she kept it in shoe boxes.

The mythology of a clandestine collection is not supported by surviving documents in the archives of the Virginia Museum of Fine Arts. Usually reticent, Mr. Pratt himself refuted the story that his wife's collection was formed in secret, a notion that may have been fostered by his known dislike of dealers, which is also documented in the archives. One dealer wrote her, "I would like you to let me know when you are entirely alone on a Saturday or a Sunday, as I would not want to examine your things when anyone, especially Mr. P., is at home. That is, I don't think you would want it."

We might wonder how an accomplished businessman could overlook his wife's steady—and regularly recorded—outlay for Fabergé acquisitions made almost monthly for more than a decade. Between March 1934 and November 1945, Mrs. Pratt spent just under $100,000 at New York City's Schaffer Gallery alone. This was an enormous sum during the years of the Great Depression and the Second World War. Simultaneously, she was purchasing a large number of Russian pieces, including four of her imperial Easter eggs, from the Hammer Galleries, also in New York. The Virginia Museum archives do not hold receipts for every piece acquired, so the total outlay for Mrs. Pratt's collection can only be estimated. Clearly, however, it was substantial enough to exceed "pin money" from even the most unsuspecting husband.

Nor did Mrs. Pratt keep her treasures hidden in a closet or stuffed under the bed. Records exist for several display cabinets at Chatham Manor. The mirrored cabinet, designed with the help of dealer Alexander Schaffer, was hard to miss. Schaffer wrote to Mrs. Pratt, "You see, I did want you to be able to show off your beautiful treasures to best advantage." The cabinet had been paid for by December 29, 1939.

It is difficult to believe that a man of Mr. Pratt's training—he held a degree in engineering from the University of Virginia— could be completely inured to the accomplished craftsmanship of Fabergé objects, with their precision parts and finely tuned mechanisms. Indeed, Mr. Pratt later underwrote the elaborate gallery installation in which the collection would be presented at the Virginia Museum of Fine Arts for the next quarter of a century

(FIG. 13). This dramatic and much beloved installation opened in 1953. It cost $25,000, a healthy sum for a museum installation at that time. Pratt also supported two catalogues of his wife's collection (Lesley 1960; Lesley 1976).

Many journalists, delighted by the collection's incongruous arrival at the Virginia Museum of Fine Arts in the back of a station wagon, have dramatized the circumstances of the Pratt bequest with a little more "cloak-and-dagger" mystery than was probably the case. A journalist for *Time* magazine gushed:

> It sounded good, but how good? Thomas Colt, Jr., director of the Virginia Museum of Fine Arts, had no idea. All he knew was that a wealthy Mrs. John Lee Pratt had willed to the museum her collection of the last Russian Czar's family trinkets. Colt drove over to the Pratt home in Fredericksburg, piled the packages in the back of his station wagon and brought them back to the red brick museum in Richmond. When he recalls how casually he treated these treasures, he shudders. When he unwrapped Mrs. Pratt's gifts he found: a world globe of topaz on a solid gold base; a rock crystal Easter egg rimmed with diamonds…(*Time* 1947).

It is entirely unlikely that Colt missed the significance of "a wealthy Mrs. Pratt's" collection any more than her husband did. The Pratts moved in the same Fredericksburg social circle as several members of the Museum's original Board of Trustees, including Corinne

FIG. 13. *Fabergé installation designed by director Leslie Cheek, Jr.,*
*Virginia Museum of Fine Arts, 1953.*

FIG. 14. *Trooper C. R. Caldwell drives a jeweled egg to Roanoke: Museum director Leslie Cheek, Jr., publicizes a special exhibition of Russian decorative arts from the Virginia Museum of Fine Arts.*

Melchers, wife of the painter Gari Melchers, and Jessie Ball duPont. John Lee Pratt was also a Museum Trustee; in 1945, two years before the bequest, he sat on the Executive Committee and headed the Artist Fellowship Committee, which he had founded.

By the time Colt served as director, the Pratts had already donated a mirrored table with silver-gilt mounts attributed to Fabergé. This gift was made five years before Mrs. Pratt's death. Having helped to pack and transport her collection to the Virginia Museum himself (it *was* his station wagon), Colt cannot have been very surprised by the contents, nor did he treat them "casually" as the journalist for *Time* averred. In fact, most of the pieces were stored in a bank vault until special security measures could be instituted at the Museum.

Occasionally since 1947, the Virginia Museum of Fine Arts has exhibited pieces of Mrs. Pratt's Russian decorative arts collection elsewhere (FIG. 14). Ordinarily her Fabergé collection remains on permanent view at the Museum in Richmond.

## SHOPPING, COLLECTING, REMEMBERING

Newly married, the Pratts moved back East, living in Delaware and New York as Mr. Pratt rose Horatio Alger-like, through E. I. du Pont and its affiliate, the General Motors Corporation. When Mr. Pratt conducted business in New York, his wife frequently shopped for bric-a-brac, an appropriate activity for a major corporate executive's spouse. By the turn of the century, collecting had become a popular pastime for middle- and upper-class women (Benson 1986). Americana then existed in a far greater supply than it does now and was much more affordable. The same was true of Fabergé pieces.

While collecting Americana was becoming quite common, we don't know precisely what sparked Mrs. Pratt's interest in things Russian. Shopping, collecting, and remembering, however, were inextricably intertwined. Mr. Pratt later recalled that his wife awoke to the glittering splendors of Fabergé at Lord and Taylor, an upscale New York emporium where Mrs. Pratt maintained a charge account. As both art and decoration became commodified in late nineteenth-century America, it was not unusual to encounter exhibitions of antiques in major department stores, whose enticing displays were theatrical, to say the least (FIG. 15).

Involved in selling art for the Soviet government as early as 1928, the entrepreneurial Armand Hammer took advantage of the American vogue for department-store-as-exhibition-venue.

FIG. 15. *A 1904 Easter extravaganza at Simpson-Crawford Company's department store, New York.*

FIG. 16. *"We don't call them secondhand anymore. We call them antiques."*

26

He made a clever marketing move that put him in close contact with women like Mrs. Pratt; that is, ladies who "were making period collections for their homes" as the *New York Times* put it (Williams 1980). The status of previously owned goods was rising, as a journal illustration of window-shoppers points out: "We don't call them secondhand anymore. We call them antiques," one woman assures her companion (FIG. 16). Hammer moved his headquarters from Paris to New York in 1932 and arranged to show his Russian treasures at department stores in several big cities, beginning with Scruggs, Vandervoort and Barney in St. Louis. By the start of the new year, he reached Lord and Taylor. On January 2, 1933, the *New York Times* bubbled, "Jewelry of Czar on View This Week...Gold Champagne Pails." A catalogue for Hammer's *Russian Imperial Exhibit*, inscribed in Mrs. Pratt's bold hand, "Lord and Taylor, 7th floor to right of elevator," gives us some idea of what she might have encountered during an afternoon's shopping spree. The exhibition comprised "crown jeweled objects of art in diamonds, rubies and emeralds; old world antique brocades and fabrics, vestments, copes, chasubles, imperial silverware, porcelain and glassware, Russian icons."

NO. 11. *A silver gilt fork, Mrs. Pratt's first Russian purchase.*

According to the catalogue text, the jeweled Fabergé objects "in themselves constitute an endless source of wonderment" while most of the china, glassware, and porcelain on view was made "in the Royal Imperial Porcelain Factory at St. Petersburg" by order of the Czar and was "never offered for sale." The range of Mrs. Pratt's eventual collection—from textile fragments to icons to imperial eggs—is set out in the pages of Hammer's catalogue for the Lord and Taylor exhibition.

Mrs. Pratt's first documented Russian purchase, made on January 25, 1933, was unassuming: a silver gilt fork with a mother-of-pearl handle (NO. 11). Although not attributed to Fabergé, the fork bore an enticing Russian provenance, "from the Winter Palace Collection in St. Petersburg." Dated receipts indicate that Mrs. Pratt must have visited the exhibition several times that week, making additional purchases. These included more flatware, her first icon, and—key to understanding her initial collecting impetus—a silver Fabergé frame (NO. 12) containing a photograph of Czar Nicholas's uncle and aunt, Grand Duke Sergei and Grand Duchess Elizabeth, who was

NO. 12. *Mrs. Pratt's first Fabergé frame.*

also the sister of Czarina Alexandra. Mrs. Pratt's first piece of Fabergé, and many pieces to follow, were intimately linked to the tragic fortunes of the last Russian Czar and his family. The frame commemorated the Duke's service as governor-general of Moscow from 1891 to 1904. He was assassinated the following year.

Mrs. Pratt continued to make modest acquisitions, such as her Valentine's Day purchase of a silver gilt and enamel caviar spoon, rescued from the Alexander Palace at Tsarskoe Selo outside St. Petersburg. As a group, these early purchases indicate that her first interest in Russian decorative arts was romantic and associative, not sumptuary. Over time, the quality of her buying suggests that she augmented her historical bent with a concern for aesthetics, but the antiquarianism first manifested in early 1933 was never supplanted.

Originally scheduled to last three weeks, Hammer's exhibition at Lord and Taylor went on and on, replenished from time to time out of his ample stock. On October 31, 1933, only days before the United States government officially recognized the U.S.S.R., Mrs. Pratt

NO. 13. *Mrs. Pratt began the year 1934 by collecting a golden column.*

acquired what was probably her first imperial Easter egg, the *Red Cross Egg with Miniature Portraits* (NO. 5). By this time, Hammer's descriptions, many of which survive in the Virginia Museum's archives, were typed on special stationery with Lord and Taylor on the letterhead rather than Hammer's offices at 3 East 52nd Street.

Two important works listed in the Hammer catalogue found their way into Mrs. Pratt's collection: the 1907 gold column with the Czar's miniature portrait (NO. 13) and the 1912 lapis lazuli imperial *Czarevich Egg* (NO. 4), which must have lost its original stand before Hammer brought it out of Russia (FIG. 17). Mrs. Pratt purchased the column on January 4, 1934. Existing documents let us date the purchase of her second imperial Easter egg sometime between the fall of 1933 and the spring of 1934.

Hammer particularly treasured this gold-encrusted extravaganza, the sole imperial egg pictured in his sparsely illustrated best seller, *The Quest of the Romanoff Treasure* (Hammer 1932). One of only sixteen plates in the 241-page book, it is featured as "the famous diamond and lapis Easter egg," competing with such full-page illustrations

FIG. 17. *The **Czarevich** Egg, shown with its original, now lost, stand.*

FIG. 18. *The imperial Russian crown dating to Catherine the Great.*

as *The Imperial Crown of the Romanoffs, The Author's Passport in Russia,* and *Governor Receiving Tractors.* Hammer also illustrated the gold column. And while she did not purchase the Romanov imperial crown, with its 763 carats of pearls and 3,000 diamonds, topped by "the largest ruby in the world," her acquisition of a large brooch similar in shape and materials further argues for the impact of published objects on Mrs. Pratt's thinking (FIG. 18, NO. 14).

Mrs. Pratt bypassed the *Danish Palace Egg with Ten Miniatures* (1895), also on exhibit at Lord and Taylor. Discussed but not illustrated in the catalogue, this imperial egg is now owned by the Matilda Geddings Gray Foundation, on permanent loan to the New Orleans Museum of Art. Mrs. Pratt may have carried with her the memory of an opportunity missed, until she finally acquired the *Imperial Rock Crystal Egg with Revolving*

NO. 14. *Mrs. Pratt's* **Crown Brooch** *by Fabergé.*

30

*Miniatures* (1896, N O. 1), a work similar in conception and only a year later in execution. Probably the last Fabergé imperial Easter gift she bought, the *Rock Crystal Egg* had also appeared in print, as the frontispiece for another early text on Fabergé (Bainbridge 1937).

N O. 1 5. *Brocades from the imperial Russian court caught Mrs. Pratt's eye (detail).*

She could not buy every available imperial egg on the market, but Mrs. Pratt was not immune to lesser objects that combine the skill and artistry of the West with the originality and color of the Far East, as Hammer's catalogue suggests. Among her purchases from Hammer's showing at Lord and Taylor was a silk *Brocade Runner* (N O. 1 5) accompanied by the following description:

> From a collection of brocades which were formerly used in the Imperial Chapels of the Romanoffs as altar covers and priests' robes. They were brought from the various palaces about St. Petersburg to the Winter Palace. Here soldiers of the present government sorted them for burning so that the precious gold and silver used in weaving many of them could be reclaimed. Fortunately, Dr. Armand Hammer heard of the plan and succeeded in saving a large number of the vestments by purchasing them.

31

Never mind that some of the saved vestments were cut up for runners, handbags, and knickknack boxes, offered for sale in Hammer's galleries. By acquiring this particular textile, Mrs. Pratt participated in the rescue of pre-Revolutionary Russian culture. Another revealing catalogue entry describes a white batiste handkerchief:

> Embroidered in brown and lace border, with monogram of Czarina Maria Feodorovna. Mendings made by herself; she was known for her thriftiness. From Anichkov Palace.

As has long been understood by both journalists and scholars, and probably by the collectors themselves, a significant part of the charm of collecting Fabergé in America was the exclusivity of these beautifully crafted objects and their links to a resplendent monarchy eradicated suddenly in a cataclysmic clap. Personal items such as handkerchiefs and cigarette cases and umbrella handles help to humanize royalty in a republic that hasn't any, but occasionally seems to wish it had (NOS. 16, 17, 18).

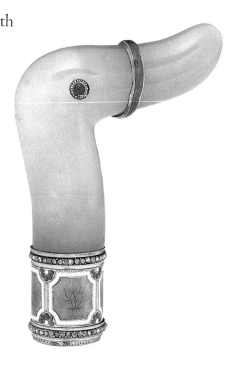

NO. 16. *Fabergé's parasol handles: A saucy duck's head.*

N O. 1 8. *A sparkling egg-shaped handle with spiraling diamonds.*

N O. 1 7. *A simple egg-shaped handle on a richly worked collar.*

At the same time, the sale of Russian imperial treasures to American and European buyers through the state-run Antikvariat—part of Lenin's "New Economic Policy" of the 1920s—had been necessitated by the collapse of Russia's feudal system and the subsequent struggles of a fledgling Bolshevik government (Solodkoff

34

FIG. 19. *Alexander Schaffer in his Rockefeller Center Gallery, about 1934,*
*the year of Mrs. Pratt's first visit.*

1984; Dziewanowski 1993). That the revolutionaries felt obliged to
sell royal artifacts for hard cash reinforced the sense that the American economic system was valid despite the Depression, during
which many of the imperial treasures changed hands. This aspect of
Fabergé's fascination would have been especially evident to Mrs.
Pratt's husband, whose colleague at General Motors, Charles Erwin

Wilson, would be credited by journalists with the catchphrase, "what's good for General Motors is good for the country."

Free-market competition meant that Armand Hammer had rivals for the available supply of Fabergé material. The chief contender for Mrs. Pratt's acquisition dollars was Alexander Schaffer, whose gallery Mrs. Pratt had discovered within a year of her first documented purchase at the Hammer Galleries. Her initial acquisitions from Schaffer, as from Hammer, were modest in both price and significance, and included an embroidered cope and an icon as well as Fabergé pieces. Among the latter was an enameled double frame with photographs of the Czar's brother, Grand Duke Michael, and his wife, as well as a diamond-studded frame with a regal photograph of the Czarina, doubtless intended to complement the jeweled miniature of the Czar purchased two months previously at Lord and Taylor.

While Mrs. Pratt's spending patterns at the Hammer Galleries are difficult to reconstruct, surviving papers do reveal that she kept what amounts to a substantial running account at the Schaffer Gallery (FIG. 19). Her first documented purchase there was made in March 1934; her last known payment on November 8, 1945. She seems to have been relatively even-handed in her trade with the two New York dealers, however. For example, she bought the *Imperial Pelican Easter Egg with Miniatures* (NO. 2) from Hammer sometime between Spring 1936 and Spring 1938. It must have been expensive—during that period she spent little at the Schaffer Gallery. In 1938, she made no recorded purchases whatsoever from Schaffer but was paying off a relatively modest sum incurred the previous year. By 1939, an exhibition catalogue confirms that she owned three imperial eggs, all of them acquired through the Hammer Galleries (Hammer Galleries 1939). Then, between February 2, 1942, and December 1, 1944, her resources were directed toward time payments at the Schaffer Gallery for the *Imperial Peter the Great Easter Egg with Miniature Statue* (NO. 3). It cost nearly four times as much as her Cadillac limousine and may have been her most expensive acquisition. If Mrs. Pratt acquired a larger number of items from Schaffer, she bought four of her five imperial eggs from Hammer, including the *Imperial Rock Crystal Easter Egg with Revolving Miniatures* (NO. 1), in all likelihood her last major Fabergé purchase.

We know that Mrs. Pratt would make successive visits to a gallery during the course of a week. Often she bought groups of things—several icons, a number of frames, three elaborate parasol handles, a large clutch of miniature Easter eggs. An avid gardener, she often purchased her hardstone and enamel flowers during the cold winter months. In a childless marriage, she favored photographs, often of the royal children. Because she was able to arrange for time payments on expensive items, she could maximize her

NOS. 19, 20. *Framed by Fabergé, a photograph of Czarevich Alexis, dressed for a 1909 state visit to Great Britain, recalls a hardstone Fabergé sailor in uniform.*

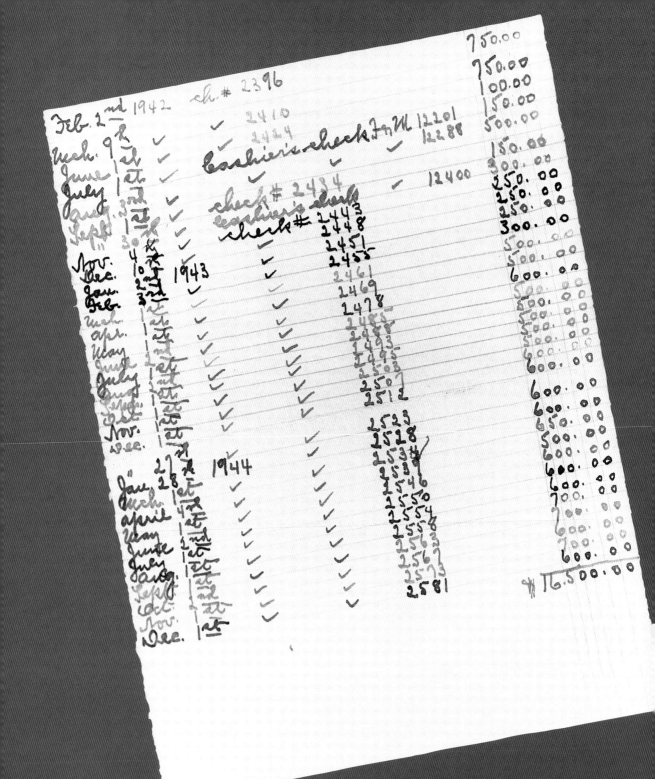

| | | | |
|---|---|---|---|
| | | | 750.00 |
| ch.# 2396 | | | 750.00 |
| 2410 | | | 100.00 |
| 2414 | | | 150.00 |
| cashier's check frM 12201 | | | 500.00 |
| 12288 | | | |
| Feb. 2nd 1942 | | | 150.00 |
| Mch. 9th | | 12400 | 300.00 |
| June 1st | check # 2434 | | 250.00 |
| July 1st | cashier's check | | 250.00 |
| Aug. 3rd | check # 2438 | | 250.00 |
| Sept. 30th | 2448 | | 300.00 |
| | 2451 | | 500.00 |
| Nov. | 2455 | | 500.00 |
| Dec. | 2461 | | 600.00 |
| Jan. 1943 | 2469 | | 500.00 |
| Feb. | 2478 | | 500.00 |
| Mch. | | | 500.00 |
| Apr. | | | 600.00 |
| May | | | 600.00 |
| June | 2502 | | |
| July | 2512 | | 600.00 |
| Aug. | | | 600.00 |
| Sept. | 2523 | | 650.00 |
| Oct. | 2528 | | 500.00 |
| Nov. | 2534 | | 600.00 |
| Dec. | 2539 | | 600.00 |
| Jan. 27  1944 | 2546 | | 600.00 |
| Jan. 28 | 2550 | | 700.00 |
| Mch. | 2554 | | |
| April 4 | 2558 | | |
| May | 2563 | | |
| June | 2567 | | |
| July | 2573 | | 600.00 |
| Aug. | 2581 | | $16,500.00 |
| Sept. | | | |
| Oct. | | | |
| Nov. | | | |
| Dec. | | | |

resources, garnering pieces that would otherwise have eluded her (FIG. 20). There is scant evidence of "trading up" or deaccessioning, and as yet no documentary proof of her collecting after 1945. There are no records that indicate transactions with Wartski in London or A La Vieille Russie in Paris, the two major European representatives of the Fabergé Workshops at the time. Like many a major collector, she patronized dealers with whom she had developed a long-term relationship of trust and respect.

## THE COLONIAL REVIVAL
## and the RUSSIAN REVOLUTION

Mrs. Pratt purchased Americana and Fabergé pieces consistently, sometimes simultaneously, and we can in part explain her twin interests in collecting American and Russian decorative arts by examining the antiquarianism fostered by the Colonial Revival.

The formation of Mrs. Pratt's Fabergé collection coincided with the purchase and furnishing of historic Chatham Manor, across the Rappahannock River from Fredericksburg. The couple acquired the house in 1931, living there permanently after Mr. Pratt's retirement as vice president of General Motors in 1937. A native Virginian, Pratt could not have chosen a more fitting estate for his retirement. His elegant Georgian manor house was built around 1760 and has rich associations with Colonial America.

FIG. 20. *Mrs. Pratt took nearly three years to pay for the **Peter the Great Egg**, one of her most important acquisitions.*

Chatham Manor's august history provides a context in which Mrs. Pratt might have been motivated to gather up the imperial Easter eggs and other Russian decorative objects that now enrich the Virginia Museum of Fine Arts.

If, at first glance, it is difficult to imagine opening the door of an American colonial mansion to encounter a glittering heap of small treasures created by the court jeweler to the Russian czars, romantic antiquarianism provides the key. The house resonates with tales of early presidents—the closest Americans come to royalty.

Erected for William Fitzhugh (1741–1809), Chatham Manor was noted for hospitality, sheltering such prominent visitors as Presidents Washington, Madison, and Monroe. "I have put my legs oftener under your mahogany at Chatham than anywhere else in the world and have enjoyed your good dinners, good wine and good company more than any other," George Washington wrote to Fitzhugh, an avid horse-racer who is remembered not only as a genial host, but also as a member of the House of Burgesses and the Continental Congress.

An auction catalogue recording the contents of Chatham Manor at the time of John Lee Pratt's demise gives us some idea of what the interior was like, and in what sort of aesthetic environment Lillian Thomas Pratt's Fabergé treasures would have been housed (Sotheby 1976). It will come as no surprise that the Pratts'

FIG. 21. *Chippendale, chinoiserie, and chintz:* **Chatham Manor,** *a luxurious home for Mrs. Pratt's Fabergé collection.*

tastes ran to English and American antiques of the late eighteenth and early nineteenth centuries—that is, assorted Chippendale, Federal, and Regency chairs, sofas, and case pieces—augmented by later revival and reproduction objects. The whole was then lightened and brightened with chintz slipcovers (FIG. 21). This comfortable mix became the hallmark of domestic interiors in proper establishments following the American Colonial Revival. Against the eighteenth-century paneling of the Pratts' entrance salon at Chatham Manor, an eagle pedestal table of uncertain origin but clear patriotism supports a Chinese pottery horse, reminding us of the eclectic decor to be found in many wealthy American households of this period.

Certain conservative circles of American painting at this time—notably the Boston School—celebrated the kinds of objects the Pratts and many others were collecting. In some pictures, such as Edmund Tarbell's *New England Interior*, Americana is prominently featured (FIG. 22). Others, including William Paxton's *The New Necklace*, let us set Americana into a larger pattern of sophisticated international materialism (FIG. 23). The model wearing the Chinese silk jacket slumps back, almost obscuring the turned Windsor armchair in which she sits. Her companion's hat and cloak cover most of the Queen Anne or Chippendale side chair in the lower right-hand corner of the composition. Paxton's ladies examine a piece of jewelry with the rapt attention Mrs. Pratt might have brought to her consideration of the Russian pendants, necklaces, and rings added to her collection. With its gilt mounts, Paxton's fall-front desk would be as much at home in St. Petersburg or Paris as in the artist's Boston studio. The large black-and-gilt-framed painting

FIG. 22. *American furniture fills Edmund Charles Tarbell's* **New England Interior,** *about 1906. Courtesy, The Museum of Fine Arts, Boston.*

42

leaning against a tapestry-covered wall typifies the steady stream of Old Master pictures and hangings flowing from the mansions and palaces of Europe to the houses of wealthy American collectors. The market was especially strong at the turn of the century.

In general, the arts of the past were seen as a soothing antidote to the often shocking social and economic turmoil of the period. Strikes at General Motors may have had a more immediate impact upon Mrs. Pratt than the Russian Revolution—at least surviving correspondence gives that impression. However, her house on the Rappahannock certainly provided both comfort and shelter in an era of unprecedented economic, social, and political change.

Pieces of Americana left to the Virginia Museum of Fine Arts in Mrs. Pratt's will reveal the same antiquarian's appetite for objects that she satisfied with her Fabergé collection.

FIG. 23. *European antiques appear in William McGregor Paxton's* **The New Necklace,** *1910. Courtesy, The Museum of Fine Arts, Boston.*

43

A mahogany dressing table, billed as "the finest example of William Savery's work," was also said to have been George Washington's.

Neither story is true. A thoroughly modern silver bowl was thought to have belonged to William Fitzhugh, for whom Chatham Manor was originally built two centuries before the bowl actually was made. Mrs. Pratt also purchased a number of portraits, including a depiction of Fitzhugh's mother attributed to Charles Bridges. That some of these pieces have not survived changes in taste or have failed to withstand scholarly scrutiny does not detract from the collector's original purpose: to surround herself with American art that in some way was linked to Chatham Manor, her own particular country seat.

Not all of Mrs. Pratt's Fabergé objects are currently accepted as genuine today. But half a century ago, Western connoisseurship of these pieces was in its infancy, while antiquarianism had the upper hand. In such an atmosphere, her attraction to pre-revolutionary Russian arts makes considerable sense. Both the authentic *Dandelion-Seed Ball* and the spurious *Tibetan Poppy* in Mrs. Pratt's garden of hardstone flowers fit neatly into the historicizing matrix that governed her collecting: each was accompanied by a Russian imperial family provenance (NOS. 21, 22).

NOS. 21, 22. *Not all of Mrs. Pratt's hardstone flowers were by Fabergé: the true* **Dandelion-Seed Ball** *and the false* **Tibetan Poppy.**

One important imperial jewel from the Pratt collection seems particularly expressive of the collector's antiquarian interests. The Easter gift that first struck Mrs. Pratt's fancy was the *Imperial Red Cross Egg with Miniature Portraits*. Its resonance with Chatham Manor lies in both its topical subject and its emotional appeal.

Chatham Manor survived the Civil War, supposedly because General Lee, who met and wooed his bride there, refused to shell the house, although it was by then the Union headquarters from whence Generals Sumner, Burnside, and McDowell launched their devastating Fredericksburg and Peninsula campaigns. An eloquently stark photograph by Matthew Brady records the manor at this time (FIG. 24).

FIG. 25. *Nurse Clara Barton, founder of the American Red Cross, wears a tiny emblem.*

NO. 5. *Similar crosses crown portraits of the Romanov nurses, hidden inside Fabergé's* **Imperial Red Cross Egg.**

Certainly not the most beautiful of Fabergé's creations, the *Red Cross Egg* (NO. 5) was made during another devastating war, the First World War, which eroded the last vestiges of Russian tolerance for czarist rule. Presented to Nicholas's mother, long the honorary head of Russia's branch of the Red Cross, the egg contains miniatures of five uniformed women, including Czarina Alexandra and her two eldest daughters. Each was active in nursing the victims of strife that was certainly the bloody equal of the carnage seen at Chatham Manor half a century earlier.

Following the Battle of Fredericksburg, Chatham Manor served as a Union hospital. Founder of the American Red Cross, Clara Barton wrote of "the beautiful grounds of the stately mansion," but was ministering to twelve hundred wounded soldiers crammed into its rooms two days later (FIG. 25). Shortly thereafter, the poet Walt Whitman visited both battlefield and hospital, writing, "in the door-yard, towards the river, are fresh graves, mostly of officers, their names on pieces of barrel staves or broken boards stuck in the dirt."

When Mrs. Pratt lent her egg to an exhibition in New York in 1939, this emotive link with the American Red Cross was picked up by the organization's presiding officer and the *New York Sun* (FIG. 26). Mrs. Pratt subsequently made great efforts to acquire a companion Easter egg through the Schaffers, but the *Red Cross Egg with Resurrection Triptych* wound up in the hands of rival collector India Minshall (FIG. 27).

FIG. 26. *The head of the American Red Cross displays the Russian **Imperial Red Cross Egg** in a 1939 news clipping.*

47

FIG. 27. *Fabergé's **Red Cross Egg with Resurrection Triptych**, The Cleveland Museum of Art.*

John Lee Pratt was surely affected by Chatham Manor's colorful wartime history, just as his wife was. His father was a Confederate soldier who returned from Appomattox with little more than a horse. Raised under austere circumstances at Aspen Grove, a farm in King George County, Mr. Pratt went on to occupy a far grander piece of Virginia real estate than his father had. For Mr. and Mrs. Pratt, as for so many other collectors, personal history brought an extra measure of meaning and delight to their personal property.

In the end, history lets us understand the motives of Lillian Thomas Pratt as a collector, as well as the lasting public appeal of the objects she bequeathed to the Virginia Museum of Fine Arts. The five imperial Easter eggs in the Pratt Collection survey the story of the Romanovs from the early, happiest days of Nicholas and Alexandra to the sad privations of World War I. If some of the miniatures in these pieces touch us with their pathos, they remain, nonetheless, splendid testaments to imaginative craftsmanship. Along with the imperial eggs, Mrs. Pratt's bejeweled frames, boxes and handles, hardstone flowers and figures, and even old photographs (NO. 23) let us contemplate splendors that few can experience firsthand. Imperial courts are scarce in the late twentieth century, but at least some of their treasures survive intact. The public museum that Mrs. Pratt chose to enrich with her collection is itself like a giant Fabergé egg, filled with surprising treasures.

NO. 23. *Mrs. Pratt, like Czar Alexander II, loved framed photographs.*

# CHAPTER 2

# FIVE FABULOUS FABERGÉ EGGS

Mrs. Pratt gathered her Easter eggs in the following order: *Red Cross Egg* (1933); *Czarevich Egg* (1933–34); *Pelican Egg* (1936–38); *Peter the Great Egg* (1942–44); *Rock Crystal Egg* (by 1945). Encompassing the history of the last Russian Czar and his family in miniature, the Pratt Collection includes the second Fabergé Easter gift given to the Czarina Alexandra Feodorovna (the *Rock Crystal Egg*, 1896), as well as an egg created for the Czar's mother in 1915 when the series was almost at an end. The Fabergé Workshops made only two more imperial Easter eggs after Mrs. Pratt's *Red Cross Egg* and its companion, *Red Cross Egg with Resurrection Triptych* (FIG. 27). Today, more than fifty imperial eggs are recorded, although some eggs, once believed to be imperial, were commissioned by other clients. Mrs. Pratt's five fabulous Fabergé eggs stand unquestioned, however, making up a significant portion of the surviving Easter eggs designed for the Romanovs by the Fabergé Workshops. The eggs are presented here in the order in which they were made.

51

# IMPERIAL ROCK CRYSTAL EASTER EGG

## with REVOLVING MINIATURES, 1896

HEAD WORKMASTER: Mikhail Evlampievich Perkhin (1860–1903)
MINIATURIST: Johannes Zehngraf (1858–1908)
A GIFT FOR: Czarina Alexandra Feodorovna (1872–1918)

A rock crystal shell encases twelve delicately painted watercolor miniatures on ivory, each surrounded by a beribboned gold frame, to give this imperial Easter gift its name. Push down on the large Siberian emerald finial, and a tiny gold hook engages one of the frames inside the egg, moving it round the central gold shaft for easy viewing.

At ten inches high, the *Rock Crystal Egg* is among the largest of all Fabergé's imperial Easter gifts. A band of diamonds edged in bright green enamel joins the two halves of the rock crystal shell. The egg gains some of its height from a stepped base of rock crystal topped with richly worked gold and enamel. The base is visually substantial, but the work is open enough not to overwhelm the transparent shell.

Czarina Alexandra Feodorovna received the egg from her husband at Eastertide in 1896, the year of their sudden ascendancy to the Russian throne. The base bears both her German and Russian

NO. I. *Imperial Rock Crystal Easter Egg.*

monograms, wrought in brightly colored enamels—having adopted the Russian Orthodox faith, Alix von Hessen-Darmstadt had been rechristened Alexandra Feodorovna. Reflected light plays through the pierced goldwork, which is further sparked by tiny rose-cut diamonds, some of them set into tiny crowns. The overall form of egg and base are repeated by the translucent emerald finial, perched atop a small gold cup edged with diamonds and striped with white enamel.

For the interior of the egg, Danish-born court painter Johannes Zehngraf created a miniature revolving picture-album with tiny souvenirs of parks and palaces scattered from Germany to Great Britain to Russia. Each locale held special memories for Nicholas and Alexandra, recalling the romantic early days of their courtship and marriage. The buildings have been identified as follows:

VIEW 1. **New Palace (Neue Palais), Darmstadt.**

Princess Alix von Hessen-Darmstadt, future Empress of Russia, was born in this house, built for her mother, Princess Alice, who reported to *her* mother, Great Britain's Queen Victoria, that Alix was "a sweet, merry little person, always laughing and a dimple in one cheek" (Buxhoeveden 1928). The New Palace was made as much like an English house as possible, helping to account for Alix's decidedly British taste.

VIEW 2. **Kranichstein, Hesse.**

A nearby castle where Alix, one of seven children, sometimes summered during her youth. "It is easy to picture the band of merry, high-spirited children romping in the suites of old-fashioned rooms at Kranichstein, racing in the park under the oaks, standing in deep admiration before the ancient winding staircase on which the picture

VIEW 1.
*New Palace, Darmstadt.*

VIEW 2.
*Kranichstein, Hesse.*

VIEW 3.
*Old Grand Ducal Palace,*
*Darmstadt.*

56

VIEW 7.
*Winter Palace, St. Petersburg.*

VIEW 8.
*Wolfsgarten, Hesse.*

VIEW 9.
*Palace Church, Coburg.*

VIEW 4.
*Rosenau, Coburg.*

VIEW 5.
*Alexander Palace,*
*Tsarskoe Selo.*

VIEW 6.
*Anichkov Palace,*
*St. Petersburg.*

57

VIEW 10.
*Windsor Palace, near London.*

VIEW 11.
*Balmoral, Scotland.*

VIEW 12.
*Osborne House, Isle of Wight.*

of a life-sized stag commemorated the spot where a real stag once sought refuge from a Landgrave [a nobleman hunting] of the old days," wrote one of Alexandra's biographers (Buxhoeveden 1928).

### VIEW 3. Old Grand Ducal Palace (Altes Palais), Darmstadt.

Set in a green park, this palace was the official seat of Alix's father, Ludwig IV, Grand Duke of Hesse. Alix's mother, Princess Alice, died when the little princess was only six; so Alix left the New Palace to spend much of her childhood here.

### VIEW 4. Rosenau, Coburg.

On April 9, 1894, the day after their engagement, the ecstatic Nicholas took Alexandra for a country drive, recalling in his diary, "We drove together in the pony-cart to Rosenau. I held the reins. Wonderful . . ." (Poliakoff 1927).

### VIEW 5. Alexander Palace, Tsarskoe Selo.

Alix was 17 when she went to Russia in 1889 to visit her elder sister Ella (Elizabeth), who had married Grand Duke Sergei, uncle to Nicholas. Much enamoured of the Hessian princess, the 21-year-old Czarevich honored his future bride with a tea dance at this palace, about twelve miles outside of St. Petersburg. After their marriage, the Alexander Palace at Tsarskoe Selo became the favorite winter residence of Nicholas and Alexandra.

### VIEW 6. Anichkov Palace, St. Petersburg.

Avoiding the vast, inhospitable Winter Palace erected by their forebears, Nicholas's parents, Czar Alexander III and Empress Maria Feodorovna, lived in this relatively small palace on the Nevsky Prospect when resident in St. Petersburg. Following her marriage on November 14, 1894, Alix spent her first Russian winter here under her mother-in-law's roof. Nicholas recalled in his diary, "In the courtyard of the Anichkov Palace we received the salute of a guard of honour. . . . Mamma was waiting in our rooms to present us with the bread and salt" (Poliakoff 1927).

VIEW 7. **Winter Palace, St. Petersburg.**

Nicholas and Alexandra were married here, she wearing a glittering old-fashioned court dress of silver brocade, cloth of gold, and ermine; he in the dashing boots and uniform of a Hussar. George, Duke of York, wrote back to England, "I think Nicky is a very lucky man to have got such a lovely and charming wife and I must say I never saw two people more in love with each other or happier than they are" (Massie 1968). The Winter Palace that Nicholas and Alexandra knew was the fourth such to be raised along the Neva River. The crowning achievement of Italian architect Count Bartolomeo Francesco Rastrelli (1700–1771), the Winter Palace was completed by 1762. Originally turquoise-blue and white, it was later painted the dull red that Zehngraf shows us in his miniature for the *Rock Crystal Egg*. Visitors to St. Petersburg today will find the Winter Palace repainted sea-green and white.

VIEW 8. **Wolfsgarten, Hesse.**

This grand ducal castle near Darmstadt was used as a hunting lodge where Alix's father took his motherless children in the summer. Following her engagement to Nicholas, Alix stayed at Wolfsgarten while completing her instruction in the Orthodox faith. Nicholas was to join her there, but had to go with his ailing father, Czar Alexander III, to the seaside. The Czarevich wrote in his diary, "the sense of duty, which compelled me to accompany my parents to the Crimea, fought with the violent desire to fly to darling Alix in Wolfsgarten" (Poliakoff 1927). Instead, she came to him at the Crimean Palace of Livadia on October 10, 1894, receiving Czar Alexander III's blessing only days before his death on October 20.

VIEW 9. **Palace Church, Coburg.**

On April 4, 1894, Nicholas came to the capital of the old German Duchy of Saxe-Coburg-Gotha, officially representing Czarist Russia at the wedding of Alix's brother Ernest to Victoria, daughter of Alfred, Duke of Saxe-Coburg-Gotha. The wedding took place in this church. Meanwhile, the young heir to the Russian throne used his diplomatic visit to press his suit for Alix's hand. By April 8, Alix had consented to marry Nicholas.

VIEW 10. **Windsor Palace, near London.**

As the primary residence of her grandmother, Queen Victoria, Windsor Palace was a familiar part of the future Russian empress's childhood. Following their engagement, Alix's fiancé traveled to Windsor, remarking in his diary for July 12, 1894, "I slept remarkably well, waking at 9 o'clock, when Alix called to me from the garden through the window to come to breakfast with Granny" (Poliakoff 1927).

VIEW 11. **Balmoral, Scotland.**

Alix's childhood was marked by annual trips to England. She and her family would visit Balmoral when Queen Victoria was resident in Scotland for the shooting season. The British ruler indulged her many grandchildren, and the young Alix was fond of visits to "the merchants," a small shop between Abergeldie and Balmoral, where sweets, notepaper, and other small treasures were to be had. In October 1896, having recently received a somewhat more resplendent treasure—the *Rock Crystal Egg*—the new empress of Russia returned to Balmoral with Czar Nicholas on the maiden voyage of the imperial yacht *Standart*.

VIEW 12. **Osborne House, Isle of Wight.**

Following his engagement, Nicholas cruised to Britain in the imperial yacht *Polar Star* to visit his fiancée and her grandmother, Queen Victoria, during the summer of 1894. He was at Osborne House in June, writing in his diary for June 19, "I like the house and the situation very much. The view from the windows on the Sound and towards the other side is extraordinarily pretty. After lunch I made myself comfortable in the rooms downstairs; Alix is on the floor above."

# IMPERIAL PELICAN EASTER EGG
## with MINIATURES, 1897

HEAD WORKMASTER: Mikhail Evlampievich Perkhin (1860–1903)
MINIATURIST: Johannes Zehngraf (1858–1908)
A GIFT FOR: Dowager Empress Maria Feodorovna (1847–1928)

Perched majestically upon its original stand, which is modeled on a Roman furniture form, the *Pelican Egg* presses the past into the service of imperial noblesse oblige. The entire egg is a visual allegory celebrating charity and good works. The sculptured and enameled pelican nesting on the top is an ancient symbol of self-sacrifice. Raising her diamond-studded wings, the mother pelican protects her little nestlings—as they clamor for food, she plucks at her own breast to feed them. The red-gold shell is engraved with garlands, boughs, and laurel wreaths. Near the top of the shell, an engraving of the pelican family repeats the sculptural motif, while an inscription on the rose-gold exterior reads, "Visit our vineyards, O Lord, and we shall live in Thee."

The "little nestlings" in this case were actually the daughters of the aristocracy. Engraved on the shell are celebratory dates 1797–1897. Following the coronation of Czar Paul I in 1796, a "Society for Bringing Up the Young Ladies of Noble Families" was headed by his wife, Maria Feodorovna (1736–1798). In 1797, it became

NO. 2. *Imperial Pelican Easter Egg.*

the official "Department of Institutions of the Empress Maria," with various educational entities under its wing.

The mother of Czar Nicholas II, for whom the *Pelican Egg* was made, was also named Maria Feodorovna (1847–1928), and she, too, was interested in charitable works.

Most of Fabergé's Easter eggs contain separate surprises that move within the shell or can be taken out completely. But the entire *Pelican Egg* interior is itself the surprise. The egg unfolds in vertical slices to become a screen of golden oval frames, each rimmed with seed pearls. The frames hold a series of eight miniature watercolors on ivory. Each shows a building that once housed some kind of educational institution for women of privilege. An engraved gold panel on the back of each oval names the institution located in the building depicted. Engraved symbols of science and the arts embellish an oval leaf that folds out to serve as an easel supporting the nest of pelicans when the egg is open. From left to right, the buildings are as follows:

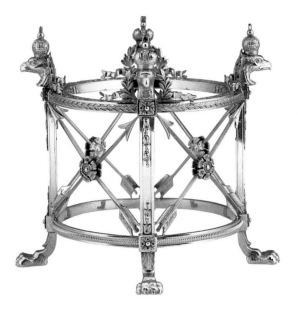

VIEW I.

*Xenia Institute.*

VIEW 2.

*Nicholas Orphanage.*

VIEW 3.

*Patriotic Institute.*

VIEW 4.

*Smolny Institute.*

VIEW 5.
*Catherine Institute.*

VIEW 6.
*Pavlov Institute.*

VIEW 7.
*St. Petersburg Orphanage
of Nicholas.*

VIEW 8.
*Elizabeth Institute.*

VIEW 1. **Xenia Institute.**

Situated in the Nicholas (Nikolaevsky) Palace (1853–1861), the Xenia Institute was founded in 1894. Also known as the Kseniinsky Boarding School, the institute was founded by Czar Alexander III in honor of his eldest daughter, the Grand Duchess Xenia (Ksenia) Aleksandrovna, as an educational facility for the daughters of noble families. After it was closed during the 1917 revolution, the structure was renamed the Labor Palace, and housed the Trade Union Council.

VIEW 2. **Nicholas Orphanage.**

Over the gates of the Razumovsky Palace, a figure of a pelican tearing its breast to feed its nestlings symbolizes the same ideals of charity as the *Pelican Egg* itself. The Razumovsky Palace as it appears here dates from 1831–34, but the site had already undergone numerous changes by 1798, when the palace was given to the Treasury. In 1837, a Foundling Hospital established there was succeeded by the Nicholas (Nikolaevsky) Orphanage for girls. Standing on the Moika Embankment, no. 48, the palace now serves as the main building of the Herzen Pedagogical University.

VIEW 3. **Patriotic Institute.**

This educational facility for women on Vasilievsky Island occupied a classical building erected in 1824–25 by A. A. Mikhailov, Jr. During the early 1830s, the Russian writer Nikolai Gogol taught there. After 1921 the building was given over to the Leningrad Energy Technical College (Tekhnicum).

VIEW 4. **Smolny Institute.**

Named after the early tar yards that provided pitch for ship-building in St. Petersburg, the Smolny Convent occupied a site on the Neva River above the Peter Paul Fortress. Catherine the Great acceded to the Russian throne in 1764, just as the convent opened. She confiscated some of the buildings to house her Smolny Institute, a school for the daughters of the highest nobility based on Madame de Maintenon's seminary at St. Cyr. The convent closed in 1797, becoming a home for widows. The school was shut down in 1917. In an ironic about-face, the Smolny then served as Bolshevik Party Headquarters during the Revolution, and later as the seat of the first Soviet Government. Today it houses the Mayor's office.

### VIEW 5. Catherine Institute.

Intended for aristocrats of lesser rank than those attending the Smolny Institute, the Catherine (Ekaterininsky) Institute, or Institute of the Order of St. Catherine, was founded in 1798. Eventually it occupied an early nineteenth-century structure erected on the site of the eighteenth-century Italian Palace. The newer building still stands on the Fontanka Embankment, no. 36. Having served as a school and then a hospital, the building is now a branch of the Russian National Library.

### VIEW 6. Pavlov Institute.

Established in 1836, the Pavlov (Pavlovsky) Women's Institute originally served the daughters of military officers and soldiers, but in 1849, by order of Czar Nicholas I, it was restricted to all but the daughters of noble families. The building seen here was designed by R. A. Zheliazevich, and built between 1845 and 1850 on Znamenskaia Street, no. 8, near the Catherine Institute. It continues to serve as an educational institution today.

### VIEW 7. St. Petersburg Orphanage of Nicholas.

Founded in 1837, this was a juvenile department of the Nicholas Orphanage. It stood on the Schlisselburg Prospect, the village of the Porcelain Factory, no. 125.

### VIEW 8. Elizabeth Institute.

This charitable institution on Vasiliev Island began in 1806 when a colonel's wife opened an orphanage where daughters of low-ranking officers could learn needlework and other genteel handicrafts to support themselves. The organization was named the Elizabeth Institute in 1892. By the time the *Pelican Egg* was created, the institute emphasized teaching as the most suitable occupation for its graduates.

# IMPERIAL PETER THE GREAT EASTER EGG
## with MINIATURE STATUE, 1903

HEAD WORKMASTER: Mikhail Evlampievich Perkhin (1860–1903)
MINIATURIST: B. Byalz (active ca. 1900)
A GIFT FOR: Czarina Alexandra Feodorovna (1872–1918)

This remarkably detailed egg makes a layered but not subtle asser-
tion of political and economic success. Like "before" and "after"
photographs, watercolor miniatures occupy opposite sides of the
elaborate Easter extravaganza. Russia's Westernization began with
Peter the Great, whose portrait on one side of the egg provides a
weighty counterpart to that of Czar Nicholas on the other. A log
cabin on the back of the egg commemorates Peter's founding of St.
Petersburg on the banks of the Neva River in 1703. On the front is
a glimpse of the vast Neoclassical Winter Palace as it was two hundred years later, during Nicholas's reign. A contemporary guidebook
for Western tourists narrated how "St. Petersburg struggled into
being on its marshy foundation, despite destroying floods and
nearly insuperable impediments," before going on to describe the
Winter Palace as "the hugest imperial residence extant," enclosing
state apartments that were "the last word in regal grandeur," and
hosting court balls "unequalled in lustre and gaiety" (Wood 1912).

NO. 3. *Imperial Peter the Great Easter Egg.*

*Czar Peter I (Peter the Great).*

*The Foundation of St. Petersburg, 1703.*

*The Winter Palace in St. Petersburg, 1903.*

*Czar Nicholas II.*

Above the log cabin and the palace, the dates "1703" and "1903" are worked in diamonds. A glorious enameled wreath, centered by Czar Nicholas's own monogram in diamonds, circles the top of the shell. Several fluttering ribbons have been worked in white enamel inscribed in black Cyrillic letters to further elaborate the egg's central theme. At the bottom of the shell, an imposing double-headed imperial eagle in black enamel is crowned with two diamonds. The bird's center is a large table diamond, under which a tiny picture depicts St. George defeating the dragon. Lightsome C-scrolls of diamonds and channel-cut ruby cattails flash and flicker across the richly chased golden surface.

Appropriately, the model for this resplendent testament to the long years of Romanov rule was a French *nécessaire* with a clock, made in the late 1750s, and soon thereafter a part of the Hermitage's extensive art collection (von Habsburg 1986). The tourist guidebook emphasized the European orientation of the city, reporting "the spirit of Peter was also in Catherine the Second's reign. She imported not only workmen from abroad, but intellects as well." The Romanov success, the guidebook continued, was best seen in "St. Petersburg, made in the image of Europe," by then "an extraordinarily prosperous centre. It has Galleries, Institutes, and Museums equal to those of other capitals, and a long list of tourist attractions." Not the least of these was Falconet's equestrian statue of Peter the Great, "familiar to everyone who has seen pictures of the capital" (Wood 1912).

Lift the lid of this Easter egg and up rises a gold replica of the statue, supposedly modeled by Georgy Malyshev and mounted on a large sapphire. Gesturing imperiously, Peter the Great on horseback rears up against a sunny dome of yellow enamel to personify a regal capital on its two-hundredth birthday. "When it was but a raw novice of a city, he confidently gave it his name. Where else has a sovereign so splendid a namesake?" queried the guidebook. Ironically, the celebration of this milestone in the history of the Romanov dynasty took place in 1903, the year that also witnessed the foundation of the Russian Socialist Revolutionary Party.

# IMPERIAL CZAREVICH EASTER EGG

## with MINIATURE PORTRAIT, 1912

HEAD WORKMASTER: Henrik Emanuel Wigström (1862–1923)
MINIATURIST: Unknown
A GIFT FOR: Czarina Alexandra Feodorovna (1872–1918)

Encrusted with architectural motifs worked in gold, this resplendent lapis lazuli egg makes a suitable container for the portrait of Nicholas and Alexandra's only son and last child, the Czarevich Alexis (Aleksei Nikolaevich, 1904–1918). The goldwork covers joints between sections of stone, making the egg appear as if carved from a single block of lapis. The original stand, which can be seen in a vintage photograph (FIG. 17) is currently unlocated, and does not seem to have been brought out of Russia by Armand Hammer when he acquired the egg.

An imperial double-headed eagle motif adds continuity to this Easter gift, whose regal yet simple blue-and-gold color scheme belies the designer's eclectic assemblage of decorative motifs. The eagles vie for space with double-winged busts that turn cupids into caryatids. Hanging chinoiserie canopies, florid scrolls, graceful garlands, and flower baskets festoon the remaining space. The initials "AF" and the date "1912" can be seen under a large table diamond at

NO. 4. *Imperial Czarevich Easter Egg.*

the top of the egg. These marks indicate that the Czarina Alexandra Feodorovna received the lapis egg from her husband in 1912.

The crowned double-headed eagle motif is repeated in the surprise, for the egg hides a similar bird, made of platinum completely studded with diamonds and set on a small lapis base like an elaborate chess piece. The eagle spreads glittering wings, while holding the orb and sceptre of the Romanov dynasty in its claws and a miniature portrait of the heir apparent in its belly. The eagle's split crown topped with a cross, as well as its orb and sceptre, replicates in miniature the Romanov crown jewels, including the imperial crown made in the eighteenth century by Posier, court jeweler to Catherine the Great. Hundreds of tiny

rose-cut diamonds set into the eagle frame might have reminded the Fabergé Workshop craftsmen of the more than three thousand diamonds in the imperial crown, or of the massive Orlov diamond, weighing almost two hundred carats and topped with yet another double-headed eagle, on the Romanov imperial sceptre.

The unsigned miniature portrait of the Czarevich in a sailor suit survives, but has suffered damage, so that the Virginia Museum of Fine Arts has replaced the original double-sided watercolor on ivory with an archival photograph. Within the lapis shell, a golden disc engraved like a rose window provides a platform on which the surprise rests, held in place by two pairs of golden brackets. Underneath, on the shell's exterior, a trio of robust anthemia surrounds an opulent diamond solitaire that sparkles like the prize within the egg.

# IMPERIAL RED CROSS EASTER EGG
## with MINIATURE PORTRAITS, 1915

HEAD WORKMASTER: Henrik Emanuel Wigström (1862–1923)
MINIATURIST: Possibly Vasily Ivanovich Zuiev (b. 1870, active 1903–1918)
A GIFT FOR: Dowager Empress Maria Feodorovna (1847–1928)

Deceptively simple at first glance, the *Red Cross Egg* rewards intense scrutiny. Just underneath its pearly surface, a host of engraved patterns causes the egg to shimmer with nuanced, broken light. Made of silver, the shell is divided into a series of horizontal bands edged in gold. Each band was engraved with a different guilloche pattern before being completely covered with milky white enamel.

On opposite sides of the egg, equilateral crosses in brilliant red enamel dominate the central band; one carries the date "1914," the other "1915." The central portion of the shell is further embellished by an inscription in Cyrillic: "Greater love hath no man than this, that a man lay down his life for his friends."

The Czar's mother, Dowager Empress Maria Feodorovna, had served with the Red Cross as early as the Turko-Russian war of 1877, and officially still headed the Russian branch of the International Red Cross, when the Czar presented this egg to his mother at Eastertide in 1915. It is a monumental version of the tiny red cross

NO. 5. *Imperial Red Cross Easter Egg with Miniature Egg* (NO. 42i).

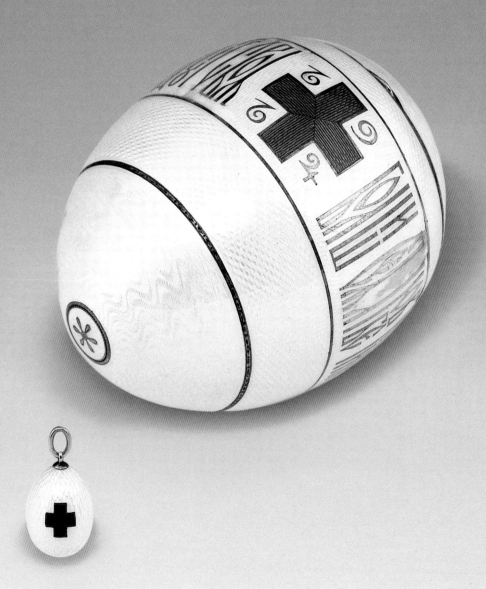

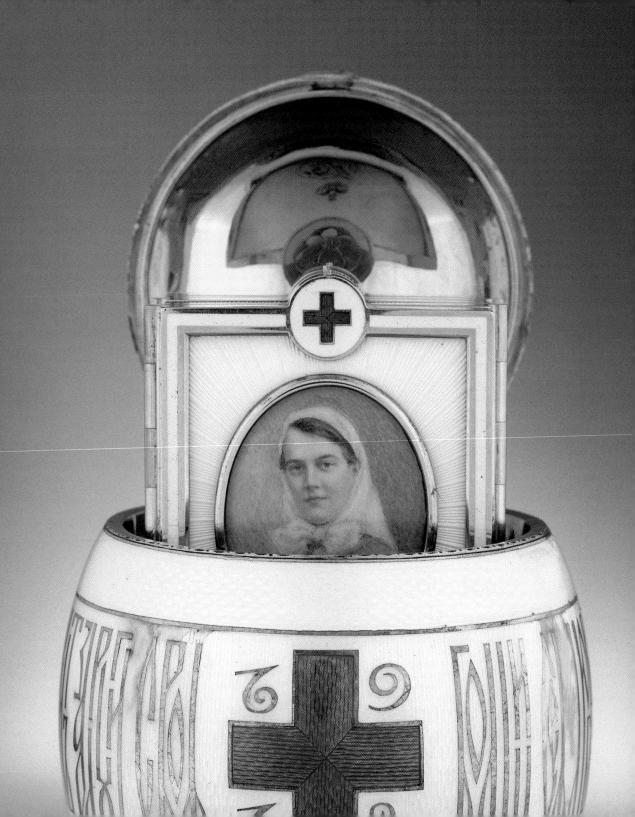

eggs that were made in profusion. Maria's monogram crowns the top of the shell, while a six-petal rosette punctuates the bottom. Only two years before, in 1913, the Romanovs had celebrated the tercentenary of their reign. But in August 1914, the first World War broke out, and by 1915, hundreds of thousands of Russian soldiers had already been captured, killed, or wounded. While Nicholas and his son were at the front in Stavka, his wife and two eldest daughters nursed some of the wounded at a hospital in Tsarskoe Selo.

In 1917, the Czar's abdication, the October Revolution, and the collapse of the Romanov dynasty swiftly followed on the heels of war. One of few immediate members of the Czar's family to escape the Bolsheviks, Dowager Empress Maria fled Russia for her native Denmark aboard a British battleship in April 1919, as the Red Army drew close to the Crimea. Behind her, in the Anichkov Palace at St. Petersburg, the seventy-two-year-old former ruler left this austere Easter egg, whose touching message of selflessness transcends the turbulent political background against which it was created.

For the surprise, the miniaturist painted five portraits on ivory, enfolding them in a gold and mother-of-pearl screen that nestles securely inside the velvet-lined egg. Each sitter's monogram is worked in gold on the back of her screen panel. Conservators working on the egg discovered small leaves of silver foil inserted behind each portrait, to reflect light through the translucent ivory backgrounds.

Each of the five women shown inside the egg wears a Red Cross uniform. As the screen unfolds, the sitters are, from left to right:

I.    **Grand Duchess Olga Aleksandrovna (1882–1960),** youngest daughter of Dowager Empress Maria, was a teenager when her brother Nicholas married Alexandra. Olga Aleksandrovna was close to the Czarina and became the most intimate friend of the Czar's daughters, who looked on her as an ideal elder sister. Olga Aleksandrovna's war work with ambulance trains took her near the front lines. Escaping the revolution on a British warship, she stayed in Denmark, her mother's homeland, until 1948. Olga then moved to a small farm outside Toronto, where she died at the age of 78, having outlived most of her family by decades.

2.    A quick mind distinguished **Grand Duchess Olga Nikolaevna (1895–1918),** the Czar's eldest daughter. Raised in a tight-knit family, Olga and the other royal children were sheltered from much contact with ordinary people until she and her sister Tatiana joined their mother in nursing activities and administrative work on committees of charitable institutions. In 1916, the year after this miniature was painted, Alexandra wrote to Nicholas, "Olga had a committee yesterday evening…Volodia Volch [Prince Vladimir Volonsky, Vice-Minister for the Interior], who always has a smile or two for her, avoided her eyes and never once smiled. You see how our girlies have learned to watch people and their faces. They have developed much interiorly through all this suffering [and] have the insight and the feelings of the soul of much wiser things" (Poliakoff 1927).

3.    Opening a hospital in the historic Palace of Elizabeth in Tsarskoe Selo, the **Czarina Alexandra Feodorovna (1872–1918)** "had taken up from the very first day of the War the cause of the wounded," wrote one of her biographers. "The halls and drawing rooms, which had seen the splendours of the court of Catherine the Great, were transformed into wards, where wounded officers and men were cared for under the direct supervision of the Empress. No service seemed too low for her and in an access of nervous energy she wore out her frail strength by taking part daily in operations and in dressing the hardest cases.

Not content with this personal effort, Alexandra became the active head of an organization which controlled a number of sanitary trains, field ambulances and in many other ways supplemented the activities of the military hospitals and of the Red Cross" (Poliakoff 1927).

**4.     Grand Duchess Tatiana Nikolaevna (1897–1918)**, the Czar's second daughter, was considered a beauty, but was also unusually kindhearted. "Her poetic far-away look" was not quite in keeping with her character, "a mixture of exactness, thoroughness and perseverance," as one witness put it. During the war she founded the Refugee Committee, which dealt with the housing, feeding, and general welfare of refugees all over Russia. The committee "became almost a department of State," recalled a biographer (Buxhoeveden 1928).

**5.     Raised in the household of Czar Nicholas II's uncle, the Grand Duke Sergei (1857–1905), **Grand Duchess Maria Pavlovna (1890–1958)** was so close to the imperial family that she was almost considered a daughter. Married at a young age to Prince William of Sweden, Maria soon divorced him, coming back to Russia to serve as a front-line nurse during World War I. She later recalled, "As I look back now, indeed, I can say in full sincerity that the years I spent doing war work were the happiest of my life. Each day brought me wider contacts, fresh impressions, new opportunity to escape from the old restrictions. Little by little, I spread my wings and tested my strength; the walls which for so long had fenced me off from reality were now finally pierced" (Marie 1931).

CHAPTER 3

# A WINTER GARDEN

"Flowers seem intended for the solace of ordinary humanity" wrote John Ruskin, one of the most influential art critics of the nineteenth century. During Ruskin's lifetime, growing, collecting, and naming plants became fashionable. Crossing social as well as intellectual barriers, the Victorian passion for plants encompassed the nobleman and the commoner alike, appealing to august heads of state, sentimental ladies, inquiring scientists, curious fashion-seekers, intrepid explorers, avid gardeners, and indefatigable journalists.

Both Czar Nicholas and his wife, Alexandra, loved flowers. As cultured multilingual Europeans raised during the 1870s and 1880s, they were certainly acquainted with the writings of John Ruskin and would also have been well aware of various methods for bringing Nature indoors, from the elaborate glass houses of famous European parks, botanical gardens, and royal residences (including their own), to the plant-filled conservatories and bay windows of city apartments, to the ferneries and terrariums that graced many a Victorian parlor. A granddaughter of Britain's Queen Victoria, Empress Alexandra was especially attuned to English styles; her favorite decorating fabric was English flowered chintz.

Fresh air was a regular part of the family's routine. Every June, the Russian imperial family boarded their yacht, the *Standart*, to spend the longest days of the year cruising along the rocky Finnish coast. In March and September, they enjoyed the balmy temperatures at Livadia, a villa overlooking the Black Sea. Filled with light wooden furniture and pink chintz fabrics strewn with mauve flowers, the rooms felt like a "hospitable summer home rather than a palace," as the Czarina's friend Anna Vyrubova wrote (Massie 1982).

However, during the bitterly cold months of the long Russian winter, the family could usually be found in the historic Alexander Palace built by Catherine the Great at Tsarskoe Selo, about twelve miles south of St. Petersburg. There, snow begins falling in October and blankets the ground by December. On a sunny winter's day, the drifts that buried the artificial lake and the picturesque follies of the park at Tsarskoe Selo would sparkle like diamonds.

But the sun set at three o'clock in the afternoon. Winter evenings at the Alexander Palace were surely brightened by the solace that flowers bring—not only fragrant hothouse flowers, but also glittering, jeweled hardstone blossoms created by the workshops of Fabergé and collected in profusion by the Romanovs. Inspired by flowers and plants, Fabergé's workers ornamented everything from imperial eggs and miniature flower arrangements to elaborate picture frames, elegant parasol handles, seals, and boxes. At Easter time, along with gifts of decorative eggs, came the promise of spring.

Bound by floral garlands made in varicolored golds and platinum, sheaves of bulrushes rise gracefully up the sides of the *Imperial Peter the Great Easter Egg with Miniature Statue* (NO. 3). Rich red channel-cut rubies set as cattails punctuate the egg's glittering surface. Four miniature paintings on the egg commemorate the bicentenary of St. Petersburg, founded by Peter the Great in 1703. Interspersed among the miniatures, the bulrushes recall the marshy ground upon which the city began (shown in detail, facing p. 91).

Mrs. Pratt, who collected this imperial egg in the early 1940s, was deeply interested in the history of the Romanovs. She was also an active member of the Rappahannock Valley Garden Club. One of her pet projects was restoring the gardens at Chatham Manor, her country home on the Rappahannock River across from Fredericksburg. Documents in the archives of the Virginia Museum of Fine Arts tell us that Mrs. Pratt purchased many of her bejeweled and enameled hardstone flowers during the winter months, when her own garden lay fallow.

In February 1939, she acquired a little pot of hawthorne, with berries or haws made of white quartz, pink feldspar, and red coral. The leaves are cut green jade (NO. 24). Victorian books about the symbolism of flowers abound, often citing ancient writers as well as modern literature and poetry to establish an evocative "language of flowers." The hawthorne symbolizes hope or contentment. For its entry on the hawthorne, one flower book (Carruthers 1879) quotes lines from Shakespeare that seem particularly poignant, given the tragic political circumstances under which Fabergé pieces left Russia after the execution of the Czar and his family in 1918:

94

Gives not the hawthorne bush a sweeter shade
To shepherds looking on their silly sheep,
Than doth a rich embroidered canopy
To kings, that fear their subjects' treachery?

Yet anyone—from a privileged empress to a snow-bound gardener to a casual museum

NO. 24. *A surprisingly life-like hardstone pot of* **English Hawthorne.**

NO. 25. *A golden basket set with jewels, made to ornament a jade picture frame.*

visitor—can take pleasure and comfort from the delicate plant life
that flowers eternally in the jewels, semiprecious stones, and richly
colored enamels from the workshops of Peter Carl Fabergé.

Suspended by a bowknot, a sumptuous basket overflows with
roses, wrought of multicolored golds sparked with rubies (NO. 25).
The roses spill from the basket, festooning the top of a little jade
picture frame that holds images of the Czar and the Czarina. Both
the Russian court and the design staff at the Fabergé Workshops
were closely indebted to eighteenth-century France. Light and play-
ful, the basket recalls the age of the Rococo during Louis XV's
reign, when naturalistic motifs were inspired by rocks, shells, and
plants. Mrs. Pratt bought the frame in December 1940.

NOS. 26, 27, 28, 29. *Stylized floral motifs animate Fabergé's handles and seals (details).*

96

Some of Fabergé's floral ornaments are too stylized to be identified with particular blossoms. A series of lively cut diamonds center radiating sprays of golden leaves at the base of a pink-enameled parasol handle that is as cool to the touch as a brisk summer breeze (NO. 26). Mrs. Pratt carried off this piece for her collection in December 1939. A blue-enameled handle that Mrs. Pratt chose in January 1940 bears bright daisy-like heads of red enamel; the petals are complemented by rich green-enameled leaves (NO. 27). More daisy-like flowers, this time in diamonds and gold, embellish a rock crystal seal whose lilac-and-white color scheme recalls the Mauve Boudoir at the Alexander Palace (NO. 28). "Hung with mauve silk and fragrant with fresh roses and lilacs," according to Anna Vyrubova, the Mauve Boudoir was Alexandra's favorite room in the imperial family's winter residence.

In the hands of a sensitive goldsmith, semiprecious materials can take on a heightened sense of reality. The curved surfaces of individual pearls mounted in gold on Mrs. Pratt's jade seal become bell-shaped blossoms of lily of the valley (NO. 29). A flower that grows profusely in northern European forests, lily of the valley is associated with the return of happiness. Perhaps the seal suggested spring to Mrs. Pratt when she purchased it in March 1937.

A trio of conventionalized irises embellishes a transparent rock crystal picture frame edged with gold and centered with channel-cut emeralds (NO. 30). A flower whose symbolic overtones reach back to ancient Egypt, the iris is associated with the Greek goddess of the rainbow, a messenger of the gods. The flower, in turn, conjures

97

NO. 30. *Gold and ruby irises float over a transparent rock crystal frame.*

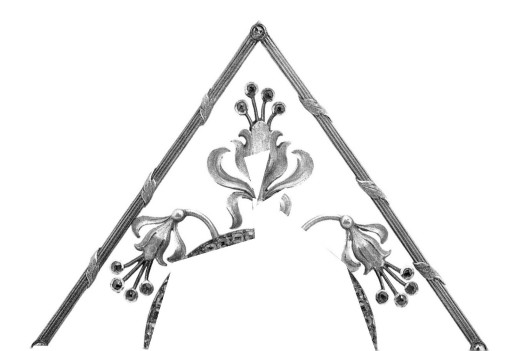

thoughts of power, eloquence, and hope. Stylized as the fleur-de-lis, the iris is intimately linked to the French nobility. Fabergé's French connection is especially evident in this piece, designed in a then-modern Art Nouveau style that was unusual in his firm's output. When Mrs. Pratt acquired the frame, it contained a photograph of Tatiana, the Czar's second daughter. The tallest and most elegant of four sisters, she was also energetic and purposeful. "You felt that she was the daughter of an emperor," recalled a Guards officer. If a favor was needed, all the children agreed that "Tatiana must ask Papa," reports one historian (Massie 1982).

On rare occasion, Fabergé workers shaped a piece to echo its floral ornament. Thought to be a snuff box, a small container takes on the same heart-shaped leaf form as the chased golden leaves entwined on its sides and top (NO. 31). The lid is so closely fitted to the box that it is difficult to open, but small precious stones stud a bright golden band of leaves that edge the opening, giving eager fingers a better grip. The leaves do not look like tobacco leaves, nor is the tubular flower that dominates the lid more than superficially similar to that of the nicotiana plant. Tinted with bright red and yellow enamels, this

NO. 31. *Nature inspired the flowers and form of this* **Leaf Box.**

trumpet-shaped blossom dominates the lid. The trumpet vine symbolizes fame, certainly appropriate given Fabergé's noble and powerful clientele.

Sometimes called blue bottles or corn cockles, cornflowers speak of delicacy and gentility in the language of flowers. The House of Fabergé was noted for the delicacy of its shimmering enamels. While rich, the blue enamel that covers the petals of these *Cornflowers* is not so dense or opaque that engraved lines on the underlying gold are obscured (NO. 32). The rock crystal container is cut and polished so that it appears to be filled with water. The glossy enamel is balanced by the glint of cut diamonds topping both pistil and stamens of each blossom. Mrs. Pratt bought this piece in June 1935. By that time of year, her own extensive garden at Chatham Manor would have been once more in bloom.

99

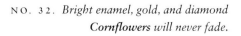

NO. 32. *Bright enamel, gold, and diamond* **Cornflowers** *will never fade.*

CHAPTER 4

# ALL THAT GLITTERS...

Imperial Easter gifts like the *Pelican Egg* exemplify the masterful craftsmanship that made Fabergé famous (NO. 2). Perched atop her glittering golden egg, an enameled pelican with wings studded by diamonds plucks at her own breast to feed her hungry chicks. The same motif, representing noble self-sacrifice, is repeated on the shell, shown here in detail. Such pieces set a standard of quality against which other objects can be evaluated.

But collectors are always hungry, and as early as the 1930s, the lucrative market for Fabergé had a side effect, neither noble nor self-sacrificing—the deliberate manufacture of forgeries. Although a solid body of firmly attributed Fabergé works is emerging, considerably more research is needed. The operations and organization of the Fabergé Workshops are becoming clearer as Russian government archives are opening their files to scholars, while special exhibitions permit comparisons among pieces in public and private collections.

NOS. 33, 34. "NOT!" squawks Fabergé's Russian **Hornbill** to the impostor **Goose** now thought to be German.

Meanwhile, the term "Fauxbergé" was recently coined to describe objects no longer accepted as being made by the Fabergé Workshops (von Habsburg 1993).

Attributing an object to Fabergé is not simply a matter of black and white. As in any area of art history, expanding scholarship leads to the reassessment of objects that once passed muster without question.

A bumptious little *Hornbill*, carved in dark smoky quartz, cocks his glittering diamond eye at a pale rock crystal *Goose* (NOS. 33, 34). The *Goose*, falsely marked "C. Fabergé" in English, cost Mrs. Pratt more than twice what she paid for the unmarked *Hornbill*. Both birds were probably intended for the British market, where hardstone animals were especially popular. The *Hornbill's* humorous personality, characteristic of the best genuine Fabergé hardstone animals, recalls whimsical creatures made for Queen Alexandra, Dowager Empress Maria's sister, and now owned by Her Majesty, Queen Elizabeth II (Snowman 1962). The less personable *Goose*, while competently carved around the same time as the *Hornbill*, is more likely the product of a German craftsman from the Idar-Oberstein region. Was Mrs. Pratt rooked?

Fortunately, reattribution does not detract from the aesthetic success of Mrs. Pratt's beautifully carved German *Bloodhound*, acquired as a Fabergé piece along with the genuine *Hornbill*.

The hound represents the work of one of many skilled competitors who adopted the *style Fabergé*, when the 1900 *Exposition Universelle* in Paris focused new attention on the firm.

Here, the suspicious dog sniffs a trail of gaudy miniature Easter eggs (NOS. 35, 36).

Probably none of this dozen is by the Fabergé Workshops. Easter eggs were already traditional in Europe by the eighteenth century, and many craftsmen made them during Fabergé's heyday. The Fabergé Workshops also followed tradition in making hardstone flowers. The diminutive *Dandelion-Seed Ball* by workmaster Henrik Wigström has delicate gold wires that end in diamond "seeds." Around each wire, a tuft of asbestos filaments is almost as convincing as real dandelion fluff. The well-cut green nephrite leaves sit gracefully in the rock crystal container, made to look as if full of water. With its awkward wire stamens, stiff flowerheads and perfunctorily carved leaves, the *Tibetan Poppy* looks rank and clumsy next to the *Dandelion* (NOS. 21, 22),

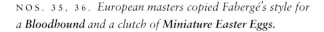

NOS. 35, 36. *European masters copied Fabergé's style for a **Bloodhound** and a clutch of **Miniature Easter Eggs.***

NOS. 21, 22. *Scale and quality distinguish the genuine*
**Dandelion-Seed Ball** *from the spurious* **Tibetan Poppy.**

making it easier to guess which bejeweled blossom in the Pratt collection turned out to be a weed.

Since Mrs. Pratt recorded the dates when she acquired many of her pieces, and since her collecting activities ceased in 1945, well before the current spate of "Fauxbergé," her collection will continue to prove valuable in establishing the perimeters for acceptable Fabergé Workshop items and those made by competitors, whether honestly intentioned or not.

# A FEW OF HER FAVORITE THINGS: Pratt Collection Checklist

**Note to the Reader:** This checklist presents select objects from the Fabergé, European, and Russian Decorative Arts Collections in the Virginia Museum of Fine Arts. The objects are numbered as they appear in the book. Measurements are given in inches by height, width, and depth or diameter.

Most of the objects were produced by the Fabergé Workshops (1841–1917). They are part of the Bequest from the Estate of Lillian Thomas Pratt and are so identified. The following objects are exceptions: No. 7, also by the Fabergé Workshops, is a Bequest of Lelia Blair Northrop; Nos. 11, 15, 22, 34–36 are part of the Pratt Collection but are not Fabergé pieces. Nos. 11 and 15 are Russian in origin; Nos. 22 and 34–36 are by unknown European makers, in the style of Fabergé.

Fabergé pieces bear the marks "Fabergé" (objects made in St. Petersburg), "K Fabergé" (Moscow objects), or the initials "KF" (usually Moscow objects), stamped or engraved in Cyrillic, translated and italicized here. St. Petersburg objects also bear the initials of Fabergé's workmasters, which are noted. State hallmarks on the objects (assay marks of St. Petersburg or Moscow, with the assay masters' initials) are noted where legible. Russian metal standards, inventory numbers, dealer marks, and import marks have not been recorded here.

### 1. Imperial Rock Crystal Easter Egg
Rock crystal, diamonds, gold, enamel, cabochon emerald, 1896
9 3/4 by 3 7/8 in.
**Marks:** Initials of workmaster Mikhail Perkhin (1860–1903), assay mark of St. Petersburg before 1896
**Miniatures:** Watercolor on ivory; all but two signed *Zehngraf*
**Pratt, Accession No.:** 47.20.32

### 2. Imperial Pelican Easter Egg
Red gold, diamonds, enamel, pearls, 1897
4 by 2 1/8 in. (without stand)
5 1/4 by 2 15/16 in. (with stand)
**Marks:** *Fabergé*. Initials of workmaster Mikhail Perkhin (1860–1903), assay mark of St. Petersburg before 1896. Stand: *Fabergé*
**Miniature folding panels:** Watercolor on ivory; signed *Zehngraf*
**Pratt, Accession No.:** 47.20.35

### 3. Imperial Peter the Great Easter Egg
Red, green, and yellow gold, platinum, diamonds, rubies, sapphire, enamel, rock crystal, 1903
4 3/8 by 3 1/4 in.
**Marks:** Engraved *K. Fabergé 1903*. Initials of workmaster Mikhail Perkhin (1860–1903), assay mark of St. Petersburg 1896–1908
**Miniatures:** Watercolor on ivory; Peter the Great signed *B. Byalz*
**Miniature statue:** Mounted on a sapphire and gold base, initials of assay master Iakov Liapunov
**Pratt, Accession No.:** 47.20.33

### 4. Imperial Czarevich Easter Egg
Lapis lazuli, gold, diamonds, platinum or silver, 1912
4 15/16 by 3 1/2 in.
**Marks:** Engraved *Fabergé*. Initials of workmaster Henrik Wigström (1862–1923)
**Miniature portrait:** Watercolor on ivory; unsigned
**Pratt, Accession No.:** 47.20.34

### 5. Imperial Red Cross Easter Egg
Enamel, silver, gold, mother-of-pearl, 1915
3 by 2 3/8 in.
**Marks:** Engraved *Fabergé 1915*. Initials of workmaster Henrik Wigström (1862–1923), assay mark of St. Petersburg 1908–1917
**Miniature portraits:** Watercolor on ivory; unsigned
**Pratt, Accession No.:** 47.20.36

### 6. Scarab Brooch
Rhodolite garnet, enamel, gold, diamonds, rubies, sterling silver
1 3/8 by 1 1/8 in.
**Marks:** Initials *KF*. Illegible punch marks
**Pratt, Accession No.:** 47.20.143

### 7. Champagne Flute
Glass, red and green gold
7 3/8 by 2 7/16 in.
**Marks:** *Fabergé*. Initials of workmaster Mikhail Perkhin (1860–1903), assay mark of St. Petersburg 1896–1908, initials of assay master Iakov Liapunov.
**Northrop, Accession No.:** 78.78.2

### 8. Egg Nécessaire
Gold
1 3/4 by 1 in.
**Marks:** *Fabergé*. Initials of workmaster Mikhail Perkhin (1860–1903), assay mark of St. Petersburg before 1896
**Pratt, Accession No.:** 47.20.46

### 9. Bonbonnière
Silver, gold, enamel, diamonds, rubies
7/8 by 1 5/8 in.
**Marks:** *Fabergé*. Russian silver mark, assay mark of St. Petersburg 1896–1908, initials of assay master Iakov Liapunov
**Pratt, Accession No.:** 47.20.279

### 10. Terrestrial Globe
Rock crystal, gold
5 1/8 by 3 1/4 in.
**Marks:** Initials of workmaster Erik Kollin (1836–1901), assay mark of St. Petersburg before 1896
**Pratt, Accession No.:** 47.20.285

### 11. Fork
Russian, late 19th century
Silver gilt, mother of pearl
**Marks:** None
**Pratt, Accession No.:** 47.20.381

### 12. Octagonal Frame
Silver, enamel; ivory back
7 1/2 by 6 15/16 by 3/4 in.
**Marks:** Initials *KF*. Assay mark of St. Petersburg 1896–1908, initials of assay master Iakov Liapunov
**Photograph:** Grand Duke Sergei and Grand Duchess Elizabeth
**Pratt, Accession No.:** 47.20.355

### 13. Imperial Column Frame with Miniature Portrait
Gold, diamonds
6 by 1 15/16 in.
**Marks:** *Fabergé*. Initials of workmaster Henrik Wigström (1862–1923), assay mark of St. Petersburg 1896–1908
**Pratt, Accession No.:** 47.20.303
**Miniature Portrait:** Nicholas II, watercolor on ivory, 2 3/16 by 1 3/8 in., unsigned
**Pratt, Accession No.:** 47.20.367

### 14. Crown Brooch
Gold, silver, rubies, sapphires, diamonds
2 1/2 by 3 by 3/8 in.
**Marks:** None
**Pratt, Accession No.:** 47.20.138

### 15. Brocade Runner
Russian, ca. 1780
Silk and metallic embroidery
**Pratt, Accession No.:** 47.20.393

### 16. Duck Parasol Handle
Bowenite, enamel, rubies, diamonds, gold, sterling silver
3 1/4 by 2 1/8 in.
**Marks:** Initials of workmaster Mikhail Perkhin (1860–1903), assay mark of St. Petersburg before 1896
**Pratt, Accession No.:** 47.20.169

### 21. Dandelion-Seed Ball
Gold, nephrite, rock crystal, asbestos filaments, sapphires
6 1/2 in.
**Marks:** *Fabergé*. Initials of workmaster Henrik Wigström (1862–1923)
**Pratt, Accession No.:** 47.20.235

### 17. Egg Parasol Handle
Chalcedony, enamel, gold, diamonds, pearls
2 7/8 by 1 7/16 in.
**Marks:** Initials of workmaster Mikhail Perkhin (1860–1903), assay mark of St. Petersburg before 1896
**Pratt, Accession No.:** 47.20.175

### 22. Tibetan Poppy
European, in the style of Fabergé, late 19th century
Agate, chalcedony, nephrite, gold, sapphire, topaz, diamond
9 3/4 by 4 by 3 1/2 in.
**Marks:** None
**Pratt, Accession No.:** 47.20.217

### 18. Mauve Egg Parasol Handle
Enamel, red and green gold, diamonds
2 3/4 by 1 1/2 in.
**Marks:** Initials of workmaster Mikhail Perkhin (1860–1903), assay mark of St. Petersburg before 1896
**Pratt, Accession No.:** 47.20.172

### 23. Openwork Frame
Silver gilt, enamel; holly-wood back
5 9/16 by 4 5/8 by 1/2 in.
**Marks:** *Fabergé*. Initials of workmaster Victor Aarne (1863–1934), assay mark of St. Petersburg 1896–1908, initials of assay master Iakov Liapunov
**Photograph:** Czar Alexander II
**Pratt, Accession No.:** 47.20.308

### 19. Sailor
Aventurine, lapis lazuli, onyx, jadeite, sapphires
4 3/4 by 2 15/16 by 1 3/8 in.
**Marks:** None
**Pratt, Accession No.:** 47.20.268

### 24. English Hawthorne
Bowenite, nephrite, chalcedony, coral, feldspar
5 1/8 by 3 1/2 in.
**Marks:** *Fabergé*. Initials of workmaster Henrik Wigström (1862–1923)
**Pratt, Accession No.:** 47.20.228

### 20. Frame
Enamel, silver gilt; holly-wood back
12 7/16 by 9 1/8 in.
**Marks:** *K Fabergé*. Initials of workmaster Anders Nevalainen (1858–1933), assay mark of St. Petersburg 1896–1908
**Photograph:** Edward, Prince of Wales (future Duke of Windsor), Czar Nicholas II, Alexis, and King George V, on a state visit to England, 1909
**Pratt, Accession No.:** 47.20.413

### 25. Frame
Jade, yellow, red, and green gold, pearls, rubies, mother-of-pearl, silver gilt
3 1/4 by 4 3/4 by 3/8 in.
**Marks:** *Fabergé*. Initials of workmaster Hjalmar Armfelt (1873–1959), assay mark of St. Petersburg 1908–1917
**Photographs:** Czar Nicholas II and Alexandra
**Pratt, Accession No.:** 47.20.354

### 26. Parasol Handle
Enamel, gold, diamonds
3 1/4 by 1 1/2 in.
**Marks:** Initials of workmaster Mikhail Perkhin (1860–1903), assay mark of St. Petersburg before 1896
**Pratt, Accession No.:** 47.20.186

### 27. Parasol Handle
Enamel, gold, diamond
3 by 7/8 in.
**Marks:** *Fabergé*. Initials of workmaster Henrik Wigström, assay mark of St. Petersburg 1896–1908
**Pratt, Accession No.:** 47.20.199

### 28. Hand Seal
Rock crystal, enamel, gold, silver, diamonds
3 by 13/16 in.
**Marks:** *Fabergé*. Initials of workmaster Mikhail Perkhin, assay mark of St. Petersburg before 1896
**Pratt, Accession No.:** 47.20.201

### 29. Hand Seal
Bowenite, gold, pearls, chalcedony
3 by 1/8 in.
**Marks:** Initials of workmaster Mikhail Perkhin (1860–1903), assay mark of St. Petersburg before 1896
**Pratt, Accession No.:** 47.20.204

### 30. Diamond-shaped Frame
Rock crystal, yellow and green gold, rubies, emeralds; ivory back
3 7/8 by 2 3/4 in.
**Marks:** Initials *KF*. Assay mark of Moscow before 1896
**Photograph:** Grand Duchess Tatiana
**Pratt, Accession No.:** 47.20.351

### 31. Leaf Box
Feldspar, gold, diamond, ruby, emerald, sapphire, pearl, enamel
1 1/16 by 2 1/16 by 11/16 in.
**Marks:** Initials *KF*. Assay mark of Moscow 1896–1908, partial initials of assay master Ivan Lebedkin
**Pratt, Accession No.:** 47.20.274

### 32. Cornflowers
Rock crystal, enamel, gold, diamonds
5 1/4 by 2 1/4 in.
**Marks:** None
**Pratt, Accession No.:** 47.20.222

### 33. Hornbill
Smoky quartz, diamonds
1 5/8 by 7/8 by 1 7/8 in.
**Marks:** None
**Pratt, Accession No.:** 47.20.256

### 34. Goose
European, possibly German, in the style of Fabergé, late 19th–early 20th century
Rock crystal, diamonds
4 1/4 by 1 5/8 by 3 1/8 in.
**Marks:** *C. Fabergé* (in English)
**Pratt, Accession No.:** 47.20.259

### 35. Bloodhound
European, probably German, in the style of Fabergé, late 19th–early 20th century
Agate, diamonds
2 9/16 by 1 1/8 by 3 1/8 in.
**Marks:** Initials *CF* (in English)
**Pratt, Accession No.:** 47.20.240

## 36. Miniature Easter Eggs
European, in the style of Fabergé,
late 19th–early 20th century

**a.** Enamel, gold, ruby
³/₄ by ¹/₂ in.
**Marks:** Initials *KF*
**Pratt, Accession No.:** 47.20.51

**b.** Enamel
⁵/₈ by ³/₈ in.
**Marks:** Illegible initials
**Pratt, Accession No.:** 47.20.88

**c.** Enamel
³/₄ by ¹/₂ in.
**Marks:** Illegible punch mark
**Pratt, Accession No.:** 47.20.54

**d.** Gold, enamel, sapphire
³/₄ by ¹/₂ in.
**Marks:** Illegible initials
**Pratt, Accession No.:** 47.20.70

**e.** Enamel, gold, diamonds
⁵/₈ by ¹/₂ in.
**Marks:** Initials *BF*, assay mark of St. Petersburg
before 1896
**Pratt, Accession No.:** 47.20.103

**f.** Enamel, gold
⁵/₈ by ³/₈ in.
**Marks:** Initials of workmaster Henrik Wigström
(1862–1923), initials of assay master A. Richter
**Pratt, Accession No.:** 47.20.102

**g.** Enamel, yellow and white diamonds
⁵/₈ by ³/₈ in.
**Marks:** Assay mark of Moscow 1908–17
**Pratt, Accession No.:** 47.20.80

**h.** Enamel, dyed agate, diamonds
⁵/₈ by ³/₈ in.
**Marks:** Initials of workmaster Alfred Thielemann
(active late 19th century), initials of assay
master Iakov Liapunov
**Pratt, Accession No.:** 47.20.96

**i.** Enamel, gold, rubies, diamond
⁵/₈ by ³/₈ in.
**Marks:** Illegible initials
**Pratt, Accession No.:** 47.20.86

**j.** Enamel
³/₄ by ⁵/₈ in.
**Marks:** None
**Pratt, Accession No.:** 47.20.58

**k.** Enamel, gold
⁵/₈ by ³/₈ in.
**Marks:** Illegible punch mark
**Pratt, Accession No.:** 47.20.115

**l.** Rock crystal, rubies, emeralds
³/₄ by ¹/₂ in.
**Marks:** Initials *KF*. Assay mark of St. Petersburg
before 1896
**Pratt, Accession No.:** 47.20.119

### 37. Pendant Easter Egg
Gold, enamel, pearls, diamond
2 by 1 1/8 in.
**Marks:** None
Pratt, Accession No.: 47.20.128

### 38. Triangular Frame
Red, green, and yellow gold, diamonds,
enamel; ivory back
2 1/2 by 2 1/8 in.
**Marks:** Initials *KF*. Assay mark of Moscow
1896–1908, initials of assay master Ivan
Lebedkin
Pratt, Accession No.: 47.20.347

### 39. Rabbit Pitcher
Silver, rubies, silver gilt
10 by 4 3/4 by 6 9/16 in.
**Marks:** *K Fabergé*. Imperial warrant, assay mark
of Moscow 1894, initials of assay master *LO*
Pratt, Accession No.: 47.20.214

### 40. Rabbit Bell Push
Silver, garnets
5 1/4 by 2 1/2 by 3 3/4 in.
**Marks:** *K Fabergé*. Assay mark of Moscow
1908–1917
Pratt, Accession No.: 47.20.213

### 41. Vial
Rock crystal, enamel, gold, sapphires
3 by 1 in.
**Marks:** Partial initials *KF*
Pratt, Accession No.: 47.20.299

### 42. Miniature Easter Eggs

**a.** Purpurine, gold
3/4 by 7/16 in.
**Marks:** Initials of workmaster Erik Kollin
(1836–1901), assay mark of St. Petersburg
before 1896
Pratt, Accession No.: 47.20.55

**b.** Quartz, rubies, diamonds, gold
7/8 by 9/16 in.
**Marks:** Illegible initials, initials of assay master
Iakov Liapunov
Pratt, Accession No.: 47.20.90

**c.** Gold, sapphires
5/8 by 3/8 in.
**Marks:** Illegible initials, assay mark of
St. Petersburg before 1896
Pratt, Accession No.: 47.20.77

**d.** Enamel, diamond
3/4 by 7/16 in.
**Marks:** Illegible punch mark
Pratt, Accession No.: 47.20.68

**e.** Gold, diamonds, ruby
5/8 by 1/2 in.
**Marks:** None
Pratt, Accession No.: 47.20.60

**f.** Enamel, rose quartz
1 by 1/2 in.
**Marks:** Initials of workmaster Fedor Afanassiev
Pratt, Accession No.: 47.20.107

**g.** Enamel, red and green gold
13/16 by 5/8 in.
**Marks:** Illegible punch mark
**Pratt, Accession No.:** 47.20.71

**h.** Enamel, gold, diamonds, cabochon emerald
1 1/8 by 1/2 in.
**Marks:** None
**Pratt, Accession No.:** 47.20.105

**i.** Enamel, gold
13/16 by 3/8 in.
**Marks:** Illegible
**Pratt, Accession No.:** 47.20.74

**j.** Gold, enamel, rubies
3/4 by 5/8 in.
**Marks:** Illegible initials
**Pratt, Accession No.:** 47.20.110

**k.** Gold, sapphire, diamond
3/4 by 1/2 in.
**Marks:** Initials *KF*. Illegible punch mark, assay mark of Moscow before 1896
**Pratt, Accession No.:** 47.20.48

**l.** Gold, diamonds, sapphire
7/8 by 7/16 in.
**Marks:** Illegible punch mark
**Pratt, Accession No.:** 47.20.65

**m.** Serpentine, diamonds, rubies, gold
15/16 by 1/2 in.
**Marks:** Initials of workmaster Mikhail Perkhin (1860–1903)
**Pratt, Accession No.:** 47.20.108

**n.** Enamel, diamonds
11/16 by 3/8 in.
**Marks:** Illegible initials
**Pratt, Accession No.:** 47.20.124

**o.** Enamel, pearls, diamonds
13/16 by 3/8 in.
**Marks:** Initials *KF*, initial *N*
**Pratt, Accession No.:** 47.20.104

**p.** Nephrite, gold, diamonds, rubies
11/16 by 3/8 in.
**Marks:** None
**Pratt, Accession No.:** 47.20.91

**q.** Enamel, gold, sapphires, diamonds
13/16 by 5/8 in.
**Marks:** None
**Pratt, Accession No.:** 47.20.72

**r.** Purpurine, enamel, diamonds, gold
1 by 1/2 in.
**Marks:** Illegible punch mark
**Pratt, Accession No.:** 47.20.49

**s.** Quartz, gold
11/16 by 7/8 in.
**Marks:** Initials *AA*
**Pratt, Accession No.:** 47.20.69

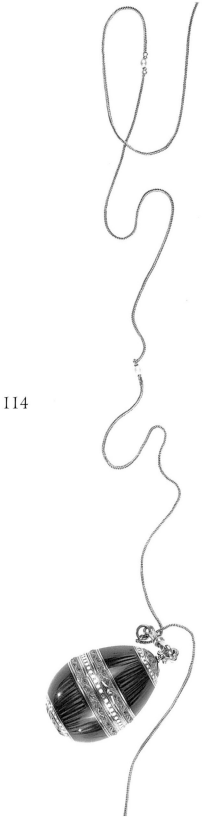

# A RUSSIAN MUSIC BOX

**Notes to the Reader:** Why not amplify your visual enjoyment of Mrs. Pratt's treasures with the aural splendors of Russian music? Fabergé's jeweled and enameled objects share a lush extravagance with the music of Russia's best-loved nineteenth-and twentieth-century composers.

| | |
|---|---|
| **Mily Alexeievich Balakirev** (1837–1910) | *Tamara*, symphonic poem, 1867–82 |
| **Alexander Borodin** (1833–1887) | *String Quartet No. 2*, 1881 |
| **Alexander Glazunov** (1865–1936) | *Violin Concerto*, 1904 |
| **Mikhail Ivanovich Glinka** (1804–1857) | *Russlan and Ludmilla*, 1837–42 |
| **Mikhail Ippolitov-Ivanov** (1859–1935) | *Suite, Caucasian Sketches*, Op. 10, 1837–42 |
| **Modest Mussorgsky** (1839–1881) | *Boris Godunov*, 1873<br>*Pictures at an Exhibition*, 1874 |
| **Sergei Prokofiev** (1891–1953) | *Symphony No. 1*, 1916–17<br>*Piano Concerto No. 3*, 1921<br>*Violin Concerto No. 2*, 1935<br>*Romeo and Juliet*, 1935–36<br>*Symphony No. 5*, 1944 |
| **Sergei Rachmaninov** (1873–1943) | *Piano Concerto No. 2*, 1901<br>*Piano Concerto No. 3*, 1909 |
| **Nikolai Rimsky-Korsakov** (1844–1908) | *Scheherazade*, 1888 |
| **Dmitri Shostakovich** (1906–1975) | *Symphony No. 1*, 1924–25<br>*Symphony No. 5*, 1937 |
| **Igor Stravinsky** (1882–1971) | *The Rite of Spring*, 1913 |
| **Peter Iliich Tchaikovsky** (1840–1893) | *Serenade for Strings*, 1880<br>*Symphony No. 4*, 1877–78<br>*Symphony No. 5*, 1888<br>*Symphony No. 6*, 1893<br>*Violin Concerto*, 1878 |

NO. 37. *Necklace with Fabergé's gold and enameled* **Pendant Easter Egg** *(detail).*

# A FABERGÉ BOOKSHELF

Bainbridge 1937. Bainbridge, Henry Charles. *Twice Seven*. 1934. Rev. ed. New York: E.P. Dutton & Co., 1937.

Bainbridge 1949. Bainbridge, Henry Charles. *Peter Carl Fabergé, Goldsmith and Jeweller to the Russian Imperial Court and the Principal Crowned Heads of Europe*. Foreword by Sacheverell Sitwell. New York: B.T. Batsford, 1949.

Benson 1986. Benson, Susan Porter. *Counter Cultures: Saleswomen, Managers and Customers in American Department Stores, 1890–1940*. Urbana: University of Illinois Press, 1986.

Birbaum 1919. Birbaum, François Petrovich. "Birbaum Memoirs," 1919. Translated by Felicity Cave. In *Fabergé: Imperial Jeweller*, by Géza von Habsburg and Marina Lopato. St. Petersburg: State Hermitage Museum; and Washington, D.C., and St. Petersburg: Fabergé Arts Foundation, 1993.

Buxhoeveden 1928. Buxhoeveden, Baroness Sophie. *The Life and Tragedy of Alexandra Feodorovna, Empress of Russia: A Biography*. London: Longman's, Green & Co., 1928.

Carruthers 1879. Carruthers, Miss. *Flower Lore: The Teachings of Flowers Historical, Legendary, Poetical and Symbolical*. Reprint, Detroit: Singing Tree Press, 1972.

Dziewanowski 1993. Dziewanowski, M.K. *A History of Soviet Russia*. 4th ed. Englewood Cliffs, N.J.: Prentice Hall, 1993.

von Habsburg 1986. Habsburg, Géza von. *Fabergé: Hofjuwelier der Zaren*. Munich: Hirmer Verlag, 1986.

von Habsburg 1993. Habsburg, Géza von. "Fauxbergé." In *Fabergé: Imperial Jeweller*, by Géza von Habsburg and Marina Lopato. St. Petersburg: State Hermitage Museum; and Washington, D.C., and St. Petersburg: Fabergé Arts Foundation, 1993.

Hammer 1932. Hammer, Armand. *The Quest of the Romanoff Treasure*. New York: William Farquhar Payson, 1932.

Hammer Galleries 1939. *Presentation of Imperial Russian Easter Gifts by Carl Fabergé Court Jeweler to Tsars Aleksandr III and Nikolai II*. New York: Hammer Galleries, 1939.

Lesley 1960. Lesley, Parker. *Handbook of the Lillian Thomas Pratt Collection: Russian Imperial Jewels*. Richmond: Virginia Museum of Fine Arts, 1960.

Lesley 1976. Lesley, Parker. *Fabergé: A Catalog of the Lillian Thomas Pratt Collection of Russian Imperial Jewels*. Richmond: Virginia Museum of Fine Arts, 1976.

Lord and Taylor 1933. *The Hammer Collection of Russian Imperial Art Treasures From the Winter Palace, Tsarskoye Selo and Other Royal Palaces*. New York: Hammer Galleries, 1933.

Marie 1931. Marie, Grand Duchess of Russia. *Education of a Princess: A Memoir*. Translation from the French and Russian edited by Russell Lord. New York: Viking Press, 1931.

Maryon 1971. Maryon, Herbert. *Metalwork and Enamelling: A Practical Treatise on Gold and Silversmith's Work and Their Allied Crafts*. 5th ed. New York: Dover Publications, Inc., 1971.

Massie 1968. Massie, Robert K. *Nicholas and Alexandra*. New York: Atheneum, 1968.

Massie 1982. Massie, Robert K., and Marilyn Pfeifer Swezey. *The Romanov Family Album*. New York: Vendome Press, 1982.

*New York Times* 1933. "Jewelery of Czar on View This Week." *The New York Times*. 2 January 1933.

*Time* 1947. "Royal Haul." *Time Magazine* (24 November 1947): 61.

Poliakoff 1927. Poliakoff, V. *The Tragic Bride: The Story of Empress Alexandra of Russia*. New York: D. Appleton & Co., 1927.

Radzinsky 1992. Radzinsky, Edvard. *The Last Tsar: The Life and Death of Nicholas II*. Translated from the Russian by Marian Schwartz. New York: Anchor Books, 1992.

Rouse 1985. Rouse, Parke, Jr. *Living by Design: Leslie Cheek and the Arts*. Williamsburg, Va.: Society of the Alumni of the College of William and Mary, 1985.

Snowman 1962. Snowman, A. Kenneth. *The Art of Carl Fabergé*. 2nd ed. London: Faber and Faber, 1962.

Solodkoff 1984. Solodkoff, Alexander von. *Masterpieces from the House of Fabergé*. New York: Abradale Press, 1984.

Sotheby 1976. Sotheby Parke Bernet, Inc. *Historic Chatham Manor in Fredericksburg, Virginia*. New York, 1976.

Walker 1969. Walker, John. *Self Portrait with Donors: Confessions of an Art Collector*. Boston: Little, Brown & Co., 1969.

Williams 1980. Williams, Robert C. "Collecting as a Business: Armand Hammer." Chapter 10 in *Russian Art and American Money 1900–1940*. Cambridge: Harvard University Press, 1980.

Wood 1912. Wood, Ruth Kedzie. *The Tourist's Russia*. New York: Dodd, Mead & Co., 1912.

# INDEX

Italicized numbers refer to pages with illustrations.

NO. 38. *Photographs of the last Czar's daughters hide under Fabergé's pink-enameled ovals with diamonds.*

# PHOTOGRAPHY CREDITS

All color and black-and-white photographs of the Fabergé, Russian, and European Decorative Arts Collections in the Virginia Museum of Fine Arts that are reproduced in this book, including the cover illustrations, were taken by Katherine Wetzel, Richmond, Virginia. The black-and-white photographs reproduced in the *Checklist* were printed by Denise Lewis, Virginia Museum of Fine Arts. Credits for all other reproductions in this book are listed below:

NOS. 39, 40. *Two silver Fabergé rabbits stand watch over Mrs. Pratt's collection of Russian imperial treasures.*